# HAUNTED
# PRESIDENTS

# HAUNTED PRESIDENTS

*Ghosts in the Lives of the Chief Executives*

Charles A. Stansfield Jr.

STACKPOLE
BOOKS

Copyright ©2010 by Stackpole Books

Published by
STACKPOLE BOOKS
5067 Ritter Road
Mechanicsburg, PA 17055
www.stackpolebooks.com

Printed in the United States of America

10  9  8  7  6  5  4  3  2  1

FIRST EDITION

Cover design by Wendy A. Reynolds

**Library of Congress Cataloging-in-Publication Data**

Stansfield, Charles A.
   Haunted presidents : ghosts in the lives of the chief executives / Charles A. Stansfield, Jr. — 1st ed.
       p. cm.
   Includes bibliographical references.
   ISBN-13: 978-0-8117-0622-3 (pbk.)
   ISBN-10: 0-8117-0622-2 (pbk.)
   1. Presidents—United States—Biography—Anecdotes. 2. Ghosts—United States—Anecdotes. I. Title.
   E176.1.S6995 2010
   973.09'9—dc22
                                        2010003576

*To my first lady, Diane*
*"Love is eternal"*

# Contents

# Introduction

Ghosts are bipartisan. They have appeared to Democrats and Republicans, liberals and conservatives. They are, in fact, way beyond bipartisan. They are universal. Stories about ghosts are common themes in the folk cultures of societies in every corner of the earth.

Why does there seem to be widespread interest, if not necessarily firm belief, in ghosts? And why are there hauntings or paranormal events strongly associated with all thirty-eight dead presidents and their families?

The fascination with presidents is quite understandable. The past and present occupants of the White House have shaped American history, and indeed, world history. Their decisions, policies, and goals have literally shaped our lives and destinies. For those who believe in ghosts, it is a logical assumption that the spirits of those exceptional men whose drive, determination, and capacity for decisive thought in an incredibly high-pressure job would eventually become restless spirits or benign presences, reluctant or unable to leave the world of the living.

Do you believe in ghosts? Or are you profoundly skeptical about anything supernatural or paranormal? Are you part of that large group, possibly a majority, who are open-minded about the possible existence of ghosts? Could your attitude be summed up as, "Probably not, but what if there were?"

Recent public opinion surveys have indicated that at least ten percent—some pollsters say forty percent—of adult Americans believe that they've had some form of contact or communication with the deceased. When open-minded skeptics are added to firm believers, a majority of Americans are willing to consider the possibility that ghosts exist.

The legend that Abraham Lincoln's ghost still haunts the White House is widely known. It is the best example of the intersection of our interest in the history of America, as reflected in the presidents, and our belief in or ambivalent attitude toward ghosts. Clearly, some presidents have had more significance to Americans than others. Of thirty-eight dead presidents, only four made it to Mount Rushmore. While those four—Washington, Jefferson, Lincoln, and Theodore Roosevelt—are honored, almost revered, others are nearly forgotten.

It is the same with ghosts. Some past presidents and their first ladies have starring roles in widely disseminated ghost stories. Others are as obscure in the supernatural world as they are in the historical record. It seems obvious that popular presidents make popular ghosts. Could it be that people are more receptive to ghost stories involving presidents they admire or at least have heard of? There is a broader, more attentive audience for stories concerning Washington or Lincoln than for legends about, say, Zachary Taylor or Chester A. Arthur.

The relative degree of interest in specific presidential ghosts is related to the "Three Cs"—character, charisma, and circumstances. Each of these qualities not only influences the popularity of supernatural tales about the various chief executives. These qualities are reflected in the stories themselves.

The spirit of George Washington's dramatic appearance at the Battle of Gettysburg, for example, precisely captures the essence of his character. The ghost, like the living man, personifies courage, perseverance, integrity, and patriotism. The Gettysburg apparition of Washington is "in character"; that is, entire platoons of soldiers were inspired by this vision because it was entirely believable, appreciating the first president's commitment to preserving the United States. For these same reasons, contemporary Americans are fascinated by this story.

Those presidents and first ladies who, in life, possessed the magnetic appeal known as charisma have become, in turn, prominent and generally sympathetic ghosts. James Madison's first lady, Dolley, for example, has become one of the better-known ghosts associated with the White House. It is understandable that Dolley's ghost is much better known than that of her husband. James was an introspective, shy intellectual—a brilliant political philosopher but not a captivating personality. Outgoing, vivacious Dolley was a perfect complement to James. She radiated charm; at her parties, she effectively lobbied Congressmen, diplomats, and bureaucrats to support her husband's policies. She was the first "superstar" first lady, setting a standard of popular appeal matched only in more recent times by Jackie Kennedy.

The circumstances of the person's life and times also influence the level of popular interest in their ghosts, as well as the nature of the legends themselves. One of the most tragic figures ever to live in the White House was Jane Pierce, wife of fourteenth president Franklin Pierce. The first and second sons of the Pierces both died of diseases in early childhood. The surviving third son was killed before his parents' eyes in a train wreck only weeks before Pierce's inauguration. Overwhelmed by grief, Jane spent her White House days secluded in a darkened room, writing letters to the spirits of her dead sons. Hers was a truly haunted life.

Probably the most famous ghost in American history is that of Abraham Lincoln. His spirit's prominence is based upon his preeminence in all of the Three Cs. Lincoln's unwavering commitment to preserving the Union and ending slavery brought forth the finest aspects of his character. In the last photographs taken of him, his honesty, strength, and integrity radiate from a face ravaged by the tremendous burdens of wartime leadership. Historians and ordinary citizens agree that Lincoln's posthumous reputation, his enduring charisma, outshines virtually every other American. The circumstances of his death—brutally slain at the moment of triumph—contribute greatly to his ghostly fame. Perhaps his ghost is so prominent in our folklore because we want to believe that his spirit is eternal and, in a spiritual way, still part of American life.

You are about to embark on a voyage of discovery—the discovery of the hidden, darker side of American history as reflected in the unique associations of ghosts and presidents. Many presidents and first ladies reportedly have become ghosts.

Others supposedly have been haunted by ghosts. Two presidents lived in allegedly haunted houses before they reached the White House. Others were haunted by lost loves, lost children, and their own shortcomings.

The geography of ghosts—the sites of their apparitions—is based on those locations of special significance to the living person. Thus, ghosts commonly haunt birthplaces, childhood homes, favorite residences, vacation retreats, and of course, grave sites.

Your journey through supernatural space and time will take you from rural Virginia to Key West, Florida, and from the New Jersey shore to the Pacific coast. Generally little-known aspects of the lives and afterlives of presidents and their families will be revealed. You will learn supernatural aspects of presidents' lives and deaths, together with some unanswered questions.

Why did Martha Washington order the room in which her husband died permanently sealed shut? Why did Warren Harding's widow adamantly refuse to permit an autopsy on her husband's body? Was Abraham Lincoln practicing spiritualism when he repeatedly visited the tomb and insisted on solitary meditation while gazing at his dead son Willie's body? Why did Richard Nixon reportedly try to talk with the portraits of dead presidents during the trauma of Watergate?

There are many other intriguing mysteries linking the paranormal and the presidents. Read on, wonder, and enjoy.

## WHITE HOUSE GHOSTS

The White House is not only the most famous house in America, but it might be the nation's most haunted house as well. The tales of those presidents, first ladies, first families, and even presidential pets said to haunt the White House are told in the chapters relating specific presidents' stories. At least a half-dozen ghosts, not related to any presidents, have been described in and around the president's official residence.

Why would the White House be haunted? A better question might be why wouldn't the White House be haunted? First of all, like most supposedly haunted houses, the White House is very old. Construction began in 1792. President George Washington, the only president who didn't live in the White House, was present at the laying of the cornerstone and advised on the location and design of the White House. It was Washington who placed the house's largest public reception room, the East Room, on the eastern side of the structure. The east, he said, was the direction of the rising sun and therefore the source of light—a symbol of enlightenment and progress and the future.

Many believe that ghosts are a form of psychic energy that can remain in a building long after a person's death. Most presidents have been powerful personalities in life and might choose to revisit the scenes of their greatest triumphs and tragedies, and in a few cases, their own deaths (William Henry Harrison, Zachary Taylor), their wives' deaths (Letitia Tyler, Caroline Harrison, Ellen Wilson) or their childrens' deaths (Willie Lincoln, Calvin Coolidge Jr.).

President Clinton's press secretary Mike McCurry admitted, "There are, from time to time, reports that the White House is haunted by mysterious appearances of figures from history, and I believe them. There have been serious people who have serious tales to tell about these encounters and there are many people who seriously believe that there is a haunting quality to the White House."

Everyone who has lived or worked in the White House is well aware of the history of the place and therefore especially sensitive to the special, perhaps paranormal, atmosphere there. Hillary Rodham Clinton observed, "There is something about the house at night that you just feel like you are summoning up the spirits of all the people who have lived there and worked there and walked through the halls there . . . it's neat. It can be a little creepy. You know, they think there's a ghost there. It is a big old house, and when the lights are out it is dark and quiet and any movement at all catches your attention."

The 127-room White House has six stories—the ground floor, state floor (State Dining Room, East Room, and Red, Blue, and Green reception rooms), second- and third-floor private quarters, and a two-story basement. It has been rebuilt twice, once following the fire of 1814, when the British tried to destroy it, and in 1948, when structural weakness required a new steel framework and complete reassembly.

The oldest of those phantoms not directly connected to a specific president or his family is that of a British soldier, circa 1814. He is said to be seen outside the White House, brandishing a lighted torch. Was he killed on the grounds while participating in the burning of the White House?

On several occasions, an unseen spirit has announced himself as "Mr. Burns." It is thought that this ghost may be David Burns, who once owned the land now occupied by the White House.

The ghost of Anne Surratt has been seen at the north portico, the front door of the White House. She is, supposedly, trying to get the president to delay or cancel the hanging of her mother, Mary Surratt, the first woman to be hanged by the U.S. government. It was in her boardinghouse that the conspiracy to assassinate Lincoln, Vice President Andrew Johnson, and Secretary of State William Seward was plotted. The evidence against her was weak. The other conspirators admitted their own guilt but denied that Mary was in on it. The nation demanded swift justice, however, and Mary was hanged along with the others on July 7, 1865, less than three months after Lincoln's death.

The ghosts of unnamed past White House staffers also appear, apparently a doorman and a butler. Allegedly, these unseen phantoms open and close doors and turn lights on and off when no living person is present.

And then there is the legend of the demon cat, said to occasionally show up in the White House basement. The demon cat appears to warn of an impending disaster. It also is said to haunt the crypt of the U.S. Capitol Building. The demon cat first appears as an appealing kitten. Within seconds, it grows into a huge, menacing, snarling wildcat. The demon cat supposedly warned of the Japanese attack on Pearl Harbor, the assassination of President Kennedy, and the 9/11 attacks on the World Trade Center and Pentagon. The demon cat's appearance warns of future disaster, but what and where? Too bad the demon cat can't talk.

# George Washington

## 1732–1799
## 1st President, 1789–1797

George Washington's ghost is said to have appeared in at least six different locations. As is common for ghosts, Washington's shade has been reported at the scene of his death and near his tomb.

The shadowy image of the great general and first president also has been reported at Woodlawn Plantation, which was Washington's wedding gift in 1799 to his nephew, Lawrence Lewis, and his step-granddaughter, Eleanor "Nelly" Custis. Nelly was the daughter of John "Jacky" Parke Custis, Washington's stepson. When Jacky died at the age of twenty-seven, his widow left her two youngest children at Mount Vernon to be raised by George and Martha. The childless Washington became very attached to both Nelly and her brother, George Washington Custis. The two step-grandchildren, raised since infancy at Mount Vernon, were more like children to George and Martha. Nelly was the joy of Washington's later years, and he called her his "favorite person."

When George Washington's ghost appears at Woodlawn, his spirit is making a very personal visit to his favorite grandchild's adult home, a sentimental, paternalistic gesture, which says much about the private man in contrast to the public hero. His ghost at Woodlawn is that of a kindly, concerned father figure, a loving and indulgent grandfather. The Woodlawn version of Washington's ghost has a gentle and approving smile on his lips. Is Washington's ghost communicating with the shades of his beloved Nelly and her family? We'll never know. When Nelly died at age seventy-three, she was buried at Mount Vernon because she wished to be near her much beloved grandparents.

While Washington's manifestations at Woodlawn have been witnessed by many people over the years, his appearances at the scene of his death in Mount Vernon's master bedroom seem to have ceased after the death of his wife, which followed in 1802, three years after his own. While some visitors and staff have sensed Washington's presence at Mount Vernon, few claim to have actually seen his ghost in his old bed.

Unlike many ghosts, famous or otherwise, Washington's spirit is not a restless one, nor a confused soul, wrenched suddenly or violently from the world of the living. His death, on December 14, 1799, was peaceful, witnessed by his family, two physicians, and his private secretary Tobias Lead. Lead recounted the great man's last words: "Tis well." These words have a special meaning to Freemasons. Washington was a well-known Freemason, having served as Grand Master of Masons in the state of Virginia. "It is well" is the traditional reply of the master of a Masonic lodge when informed that his order has been obeyed.

An interesting thing happened after Washington's burial on December 18, 1799. His widow ordered that the master bedroom be sealed shut, never to be entered again in her lifetime. Although other bedrooms were available on the second floor adjacent to the master bedroom, Martha insisted on moving her bedroom to the third floor. Why did Martha, then sixty-eight, choose a bedroom up another flight of stairs and, being closer to the roof and with lower ceilings, considerably hotter in summer? Unlike many wealthy couples of the day, George and Martha had always shared one bedroom. Why move to a less convenient, less comfortable bedroom?

Allegedly, Martha confided in Nelly that George's spirit was still in their bedroom. She had seen him, sitting up in bed, studying state papers and reports of national and international events. Was she afraid of her husband's ghost? "Oh no," she is said to have replied, "It is just that he needs his quiet time to ponder the nation's fate." Martha had loyally stayed with George during the Revolutionary War, sharing his hardships of life in the field, including that bitter winter at Valley Forge. A woman of great tact, Martha knew to give her husband solitude when he confronted the pressing problems of leadership.

She believed that his spirit was still preoccupied with the problems of the young nation, and accordingly, she granted her beloved husband's shadow the undisturbed peace he required. Before the master bedroom was shut off from the rest of the house, several servants are said to have shared Martha's vision of George's ghost, comfortably reading and thinking in bed.

It seems to be quite common for spirits to show themselves at their final resting place. Washington's phantom is said to appear on occasion at the rock crypt on the grounds of Mount Vernon, where he and Martha lie side by side. Washington is said to appear as a misty figure, glowing slightly with a greenish phosphorescence. Supposedly, he is most likely to appear near the anniversary of his own death, December 14, and that of Martha's death, May 22. On the anniversary of Martha's death, the ghost of her husband allegedly places a bouquet of red roses atop her stone sarcophagus. Are the roses real, and if so, how do they get there?

Martha Washington's ghost seems to confine its rare appearances to Mount Vernon, in contrast to the many alleged sites of her husband's spiritual appearances. Like all the daughters of wealth in her day, Martha had been trained to be a loyal helpmeet to her husband, skilled in managing a household and functioning as a gracious hostess to advance her husband's career. Martha evidently enjoyed her hostess duties at Mount Vernon but was less comfortable in her role as first lady. Washington was acutely aware that as the first chief executive of the new nation, his every move would set precedents and establish a role model for all succeeding presidents. Doubtless, Martha also was very careful to always demonstrate tact, dignity, and hospitality in her role as first lady.

Martha never cancelled an engagement related to her public duties and never publicly complained of the endless round of official receptions. She did write to her sister, however, that "I lead a very dull life. . . . I never go to any public places, indeed I think I am more like a state prisoner than anything else. There are certain bounds set for me which I must not depart from."

It must have been with a great sense of relief that Martha was able to return to Mount Vernon as a private citizen on March 4, 1797, the day the new president, John Adams, succeeded her husband. As would be expected, Martha's ghost makes only rare appearances, and always at Mount Vernon, never in a more public venue. Martha's spirit is said to appear as a misty, faintly glowing form, seated at the table in the dining room of the home she shared with George for nearly forty-one years. Her phantom allegedly is most likely to materialize on the anniversary of her marriage to George, January 6, 1759.

While Martha's ghost appears only in the tranquil domesticity of Mount Vernon, George's ghost has been observed in much more dramatic and public settings in addition to Mount Vernon and Woodlawn Plantation. Many people report seeing the heroic figure, resplendent in his general's blue-and-white uniform and tricorne, atop a great white horse. This inspiring image is said to appear often at Yorktown, the scene of his final victory as a military leader. It was a day of both public triumph and great personal satisfaction when the general accepted the British surrender of Yorktown. For several long years, Washington had led American troops against far superior forces—the more numerous, better equipped, and professionally trained soldiers of King George III. Washington well understood that, outgunned and outnumbered, he had to avoid being forced into a head-to-head battle he had little chance of winning. He would fight only when and where he was ready. Washington knew that he didn't need to win big time as much as he needed to avoid losing big time. He must choose his battles and have control over the time and place of major confrontations.

Washington's cautious strategy led to many strategic retreats. This frustrated the British generals who wanted to force battles on their choices of site and time. The British began calling Washington "the Fox," and it was not meant as a compliment; in the hunts organized by English gentry, the fox's only hope against a pack of hounds and numerous gun-toting hunters on horseback is to run and hide. In the British view, running and hiding was what Washington did best. Their buglers were ordered to play fox hunting calls on their bugles, hoping to taunt Washington into taking a stand against the pursuing army.

Washington never let his ego override his judgment; he didn't let himself be baited into an ill-timed battle just to prove his manhood. The Fox really was foxy and ignored the British accusations of cowardice and mockery of his character. Washington had only disdain for British officers' pretensions that they were honorable gentlemen fighting sniveling, amateur traitors of the crown. When British general Lord Charles Cornwallis was compelled to surrender at Yorktown, Washington had his moment of revenge. It was customary for the defeated leader to personally hand the surrender document to his equal-rank counterpart in the victorious army.

Washington decided to break protocol and sent a low-ranking American soldier into Cornwallis's camp to accept the surrender. Although there is no documentary proof of which soldier had this rare honor, tradition says it was Private John Gray, who had served throughout the war and as a teenager lived and worked on the Mount Vernon estate. And so, as military bands played the ironically appropriate popular tune, "The World Turned Upside Down," a humble private went to Lord Cornwallis. "Cornwallis wouldn't shake my hand!" Gray gleefully reported to Washington. "Good!" replied Washington. "He is not worthy of a good American soldier."

To this day, some say, the phantom of Washington may be seen at Yorktown, a faint smile on his face as he accepts a rolled-up document from a grinning American soldier. Incidentally, it is said that the ghost of John Gray, who died in Hiramsburg, Ohio, in 1868 at the age of 104, rises from his grave on patriotic holidays, dressed in his Revolutionary War uniform, to salute the flag.

It is perhaps predictable that Washington's spirit would be attracted to Yorktown Battlefield, the site of his greatest victory, but his ghost's surprising appearance at the Battle of Gettysburg is much more widely known.

Gettysburg was the scene of the greatest battle ever fought in North America, both in numbers of soldiers engaged and numbers killed in battle. The strength of 93,921 Union soldiers fought 71,693 Confederates. Over three days of fierce conflict, the Confederate casualties were 4,708 dead, 12,693 wounded, and 5,830 missing in action or captured. Union forces suffered 3,155 killed, 5,369 missing in action or captured, and an astounding 14,531 wounded. This terrible carnage has produced so many ghosts that Gettysburg may be one of the most haunted places in America.

The long list of ghost stories about Gettysburg includes at least two separate appearances by the phantom of George Washington.

It might seem perfectly natural for the great man's spirit to come to the aid of the Union at the moment when the nation faced its greatest peril, with its very survival at stake. Did Washington's spirit somehow see that a pivotal battle to preserve the United States was about to take place? The titanic battle is often called the turning point of the Civil War. After Gettysburg, the South never again mounted a major offensive and the eventual triumph of the Union was but a matter of time, although much blood would still be spilled.

In both the widely reported appearances of Washington's ghosts during this cataclysmic battle, the general's spirit clearly was favoring a Union victory. But Washington surely had an internal conflict about which side to champion, which goals to advance.

Both the Union and Confederate sides regarded Washington as their hero and role model. From the southern viewpoint, Washington was one of their own. He was a Virginian and a slaveholder. His step-great granddaughter, Mary Anne Custis, was married to Gen. Robert E. Lee, commander of the Confederate forces at Gettysburg. But in his lifetime, he had fought for the ideals of the Union, was the major Founding Father of the United States, and had spent eight years as its Chief Executive.

Both versions of the story that Washington's ghost participated in the Battle of Gettysburg portray him in full uniform, riding his white horse, and leading Union soldiers into battle, a battle that Washington's spirit evidently knew the Union must win.

In one widely circulated story, a contingent of Union soldiers had pitched camps along the road west of Hanover, Pennsylvania, having marched all day from Maryland. They were near McSherrystown on the road toward Gettysburg, on what is now Route 116. It was the evening of July 1, 1863, and the men were hot and tired. Campfires were lit and coffee was on the boil when orders came to break camp and resume marching—a great battle had begun that day at nearby Gettysburg. Grumbling and weary, the men began trudging to their destination. Then, miraculously, they witnessed an awe-inspiring sight, and fatigue was replaced by patriotic fervor. Glowing with a pulsating light as though from an inner flame, the unmistakable figure of George Washington on horseback appeared at the head of the long line of soldiers. The dazzling phantom rode ahead, and then he turned and waited until the straggling line caught up, before riding on again. Washington seemed to be impatiently urging the men forward, communicating a sense of urgency by his actions. Morale soared and the pace quickened. The spirit of Washington was leading them toward triumph!

In another version of this story, the ghost of Washington personally leads Union reinforcements into battle at Little Round Top, the hill that was at the southern end of the Union lines at Gettysburg. Washington's spirit had obviously comprehended the strategic significance of Little Round Top. If the Confederates had succeeded in "turning," or outflanking, Union forces there, they would have caught the northern armies in a pincer and the crucial battle may have been won by the South.

The appearance of Washington's ghost on the field at Gettysburg would be consistent with the actions of the living man. In life, Washington displayed great courage in personally leading his troops into battle, unmindful of his own safety. His bravery was legendary. As a young officer in the French and Indian War, no less than four bullets drilled holes in his coat and two horses were shot out from under him as he led his men into battle. His many close brushes with death convinced young George that he was a man of destiny—that God had plans for him and fate would spare him an untimely death. Washington's bravery inspired his troops then, just as his ghost inspired the Union to victory at Gettysburg.

The ghostly figure of Washington at Little Round Top is said to have held aloft a flaming sword, pointing the way forward not only for those troops, but for the Union as a whole. It is logical and consistent with the living man's loyalties that his spirit would so forcefully favor the Union cause.

Washington's political philosophy is explicitly laid out in detail in his lengthy Farewell Address. This open letter to his fellow citizens was written at the close of his presidency. A major goal was to explain his decision not to accept a third term. Ever conscious of his precedent-setting role, Washington wanted to underline his insistence on giving up personal power and ambition in favor of a democratically elected successor. Past leaders of successful revolutions had always seized power for life and founded dynasties. Washington could easily have been president for life, but he rejected that. When told that Washington intended to voluntarily leave power and return to private life, George III is said to have proclaimed, "Why, if he does that, he'll be the greatest man in the world."

Washington's ghostly support of the Union cause at Gettysburg is foreshadowed in the Farewell Address, which was published in many newspapers across America. At considerable length, he warned contemporary and future Americans of the dangers of sectionalism. He emphasized that the North needed the South and vice versa. "Every portion of our country finds the most commanding motives for carefully guarding and preserving the union as a whole. . . . Your Union ought to be considered as a main prop of your liberty, and that the love of the one ought to endear you to a preservation of the other."

This definitive declaration is a clear precursor to this ghost's flaming sword at Gettysburg. Washington was a champion of a firmly united country.

Washington's phantom made a visit to Fort Monroe at the close of the Civil War. As at Gettysburg, his motivation was rooted in his anxiety to preserve his country. Fort Monroe is located at Old Point Comfort in Hampton, Virginia; it guarded the approaches to the harbor of Hampton Roads. The largest brick fort on the East Coast, it would have been well known to Washington, having been established in 1609 to guard Jamestown. Known as the "Gibraltar of the Chesapeake," the fort was used briefly to confine Jefferson Davis following his capture by Union forces at the end of the Civil War. The former president of the Confederacy was kept in a solitary cell deep within the fort. On Davis's first evening there, his jailers saw a strange, greenish glow coming from his cell and heard what seemed to be a stern lecture from a visitor, though none could have entered the cell. A visibly shaken Davis admitted to having a vivid night-mare in which he'd been visited by Washington, who'd berated him for his treasonous betrayal of his country.

Would a midnight visit to strongly express his anger at Jefferson Davis be in character for George Washington? Of course, given his animosity to sectionalism and his known habit of angrily reprimanding anyone who failed to carry out their duties and responsibilities. Contemporary reports noted Washington's awesome vocabulary of curses when subordinates missed crucial deadlines in battlefield tactics, for example.

After Lee's surrender at Appomattox, effectively ending the war, Davis urged southerners to continue a guerilla-style war of terror from mountain hideouts. Fortunately for everyone, Lee swayed southern opinion away from such actions. He observed that, as he waged war honorably, he would be honorable in defeat. It was over.

Washington's ghost is alleged to make cameo appearances at a variety of other locations. His phantom is said to haunt the site of New York's Federal Hall at Wall and Nassau streets, where he was inaugurated as first president. Other sightings are claimed at various battlefields, including those at Princeton and Monmouth in New Jersey.

An interesting story is related by a young man who wishes to remain anonymous. Concerned that people would think he was only seeking attention, he has confided his experience only to his family and a few close friends. It happened on a recent Fourth of July, when his scout troop was visiting Mount Vernon. As has become customary, a Boy Scout was selected to lay a wreath on Washington's sarcophagus and a Girl Scout performed a similar tribute at Martha's matching resting place. Chosen to honor the president on the nation's birthday, the young man swears he heard a faint voice say "Tis Well" as he placed the wreath.

Did George Washington himself have a supernatural experience during the winter he spent at Valley Forge? Washington himself did not record the experience in writing, but a close friend, Anthony Sherman of Philadelphia, reported that a ghostly vision appeared to Washington during a time when the general was under enormous pressure. The Revolutionary War was not going well. Washington's troops, in winter quarters, needed food, clothing, medicine, and ammunition. Morale was low, and Washington himself understandably was depressed. He couldn't pay his loyal troops. The situation looked grim. Then, as Sherman later recalled in widely circulated newspaper accounts, a luminous vision appeared to the general. A spirit, or perhaps an angel, visited him in his headquarters. Washington allegedly told Sherman that the spirit showed him a magical map of the world, which changed before Washington's astonished eyes. The brightly glowing figure, which Washington called an angel of prophecy, showed him a United States expanding across the continent. The vision included a temporary crack in the map of the future United States, perhaps reference to the Civil War, but also showed a healing of this rift.

Supposedly, when Washington came out of the trancelike state, he had a new hope for the future. He is said to have interpreted this strange vision as delivering two prophecies: Washington was destined to lead his country to independence, a country that would continue to grow in power and prosperity, and the nation would eventually face a tragic civil war, but would survive and reunite.

This dramatic vision, whether it was a supernatural event or a dream produced by Washington's subconscious hopes and fears, may explain the general's renewed confidence in his cause and in his abilities. So inspired, Washington was able to inspire his army, and indeed, his whole nation as he led them to independence.

# John Adams

1735–1826
2nd President, 1797–1801

The contrast between the ghosts of John Adams and George Washington are as striking as the differences between the living men. The comparison of Washington's phantom on horseback, urging soldiers forward while brandishing a flaming sword, with John Adams's quietly contemplative shade sitting at home says it all.

While Washington's spirit has been reported not only at his Mount Vernon estate but as far afield as Gettysburg, New York City, and Princeton, Adams's ghost is strictly a homebody, and a very unobtrusive one at that. Adams had the unenviable task of succeeding Washington as president. Our first one-term president, Adams has been widely regarded as an undistinguished, rather boring bureaucrat in contrast to the charismatic Washington.

Entire regiments of soldiers claimed to have seen Washington's phantom at Gettysburg, while relatively few report spotting Adams's spirit at his home in Quincy, near Boston. There, the shade of the second president has been seen both in the parlor of his house and seated on the low stone fence outside.

In the parlor manifestation, Adams's spirit appears in the form of advanced old age. He sits in an armchair reading, perhaps reminiscing about his long life of service to his country. His expression has been described as rather sad and lost in thought. His beloved wife, Abigail, predeceased him by nearly eight years. He was frustrated by the physical disabilities of old age (he lived to the age of ninety), once writing, "I have lived in this old and frail tenement a great many years; it is very much dilapidated and from all that I can learn, my landlord doesn't intend to repair it." No wonder the parlor apparition is so seemingly morose, with his wife dead and his reputation tarnished by a controversial and unhappy term in the presidency. Adams's glum ghost reflects the man's terrible disappointment at being defeated for reelection in the bitter campaign of 1800. His words often were undiplomatically direct with more than a little self-righteousness. He was his own worst enemy, and the parlor ghost, said to glare wrathfully at any disturbance, reflects these character traits. Benjamin Franklin observed of John Adams that, "He means well for his country, and is always an honest man, often a wise one, but sometimes and in some things absolutely out of his senses."

As a diplomat, Adams often was undiplomatic; as a politician, he cynically trusted no one. "There is danger from all men," he wrote. "The only maxim of a free government ought to be to trust no man living with power to endanger the public liberty."

In contrast to the sour "parlor ghost," Adams's alternate manifestation, sitting on the stone fence outside his house, seems serenely content. This phantom appears to be looking over what were crop fields and pastures with satisfied contentment. Adams genuinely loved his home even though his duties often had him living hundreds, even thousands, of miles away. He was intensely interested in scientific agriculture for the good reason that he needed to coax the maximum income from each acre.

When Adams was appointed the first American ambassador to Britain, he was not looking forward to formally presenting his credentials to the king. Protocol required a personal visit to King George III, with a polite chat, head to head. As a revolutionary, Adams had made highly unflattering statements about the king; now, he had to make nice for an hour. Adams opened with a compliment about English successes in breeding superior sheep, hogs, and cattle. It turned out the king's hobby was scientific agriculture; they both were relieved to find a common interest.

So, it is not surprising that Adams's spirit seems most at ease looking over his farm and wearing an old farmer's straw hat. Working his farm always had brought peace to the man, and now to his spirit.

It is interesting that the ghost of Abigail Adams has captured the public's imagination more than that of her husband. Independent-minded and assertive, Abigail was a very different first lady than Martha Washington. Martha once told a friend that her husband "impressed her with his views so thoroughly that she could not distinguish her own." Abigail was the daughter of a clergyman and had a strong sense of morality. She never hesitated to give advice to her husband, or anyone else for that matter. In contrast to Martha Washington, Abigail's strongly expressed views earned her the unofficial title of "Mrs. President," not necessarily meant as a compliment. Harry Truman once said that he thought Abigail would have made a better president than John. When John was elected president, Abigail said that she would try to emulate Martha Washington in avoiding public expressions on controversial subjects, but admitted that "she'd rather be bound and gagged and shot like a turkey."

Abigail considered slavery to be a great evil and said so often. Once, when a freed black youth begged her to teach him how to read and write, the first lady had to decline because of her many official engagements. But she did enroll him in evening school, ignoring criticism from her friends for doing so.

It would have amused Abigail that her most widely reported appearances as a ghost are in the form of a dutiful housewife. She is said to be the oldest ghost in the White House and is seen wearing a lace cap and carrying a basket of laundry into the East Room. After moving into the still-unfinished White House in 1800, the first family complained that the inadequately heated stone-walled house was damp and cold. Abigail is said to have found the East Room as the only one warm enough to dry her wash in. Abigail's phantom repeats this duty, ignoring any living bystanders.

A less widely known appearance of Abigail's spirit is near the Adams homestead in Quincy, Massachusetts. A cairn, a pile of loose stones in a beehive shape, was erected in Abigail's memory atop Penn's Hill, from which vantage point Abigail had once observed the Battle of Bunker Hill. There, at her cairn, Abigail's disembodied spirit watches anxiously as American soldiers win a key, early battle. This manifestation would seem to be more characteristic of this very intelligent and public-spirited first lady than the simple domesticity of the laundry-hanger image.

# *Thomas Jefferson*

## 1743–1826
## 3rd President, 1801–1809

---

The sound of piano music is heard coming from the Yellow Oval Room on the second floor of the White House. The medley of tunes seems to have been chosen for its feeling of serene reflection. The rendition is smooth and faultless, as though the pianist is playing old familiar favorites. The notes are played softly, without dramatic flourishes, as if the pianist is playing only for his own enjoyment, not performing for an audience. The music is otherworldly in every sense. The piano and musician are but faintly shimmering, almost transparent images. While an abrupt or noisy entrance into the room will put a sudden end to the playing, a quiet, unobtrusive entry will give the listener a few more moments of pleasure before the music, the piano, and its player all fade away.

This ghostly piano player is the shade of third president Thomas Jefferson. The first president to occupy the White House for eight years, he thoroughly enjoyed his two terms in the executive mansion. His predecessor, John Adams, had moved into the still-unfinished house on November 1, 1800, and within a week had lost a bitterly contested election to Jefferson. Adams spent but one winter in the White House and was miserable doing so. No wonder Adams's ghost has never appeared there, just as it is understandable that Jefferson's phantom visits the scene of many of his life's triumphs.

White House living was very much to Jefferson's taste. He loved playing host to the famous and talented in the tradition of the Parisian salons he so admired during his diplomatic missions to France. Scientists, artists, and philosophers graced Jefferson's White House dinners and receptions along with the usual complement of political leaders.

Jefferson liked to entertain in a less formal style than that favored by Washington and continued by Adams. He often greeted guests in a robe with slippers on his feet, and so his ghost appears in that attire at the piano in the Oval Room. Some people claim to have heard him playing a violin in the White House.

Jefferson's ghost also has been seen in several rooms at his plantation home, Monticello, as well as at his rural hideaway at Poplar Forest. At Monticello, the spirits of both Jefferson and his wife Martha are said to preside, barely visible, at the dining table. Thomas had married the twenty-three-year-old widow Martha Wayles Skelton in 1772. He had already begun building the mansion at Monticello; some believe that Martha influenced the decorating of the home that Thomas designed. By all accounts, theirs was a happy marriage, a fact reflected in the relaxed smiles said to grace their dining table manifestations.

The six-foot-tall Jefferson retained a youthful, slim build all his life, despite his great enjoyment of food and reputation as a gourmet and wine connoisseur. His neighbors said that he "set a good table," referring both to quantity and quality of food served. "The wine and conversation sparkled," reported one guest, and so the dining room manifestation of Jefferson is the most radiantly happy, his lovely wife at his side, enjoying the social and culinary pleasures of dinner with friends.

This image of domestic bliss did not last long in Jefferson's life. His wife died in childbirth at the age of thirty-three. Of their six children, only two, Martha and Mary (Maria) survived infancy. It is alleged that a wailing infant can be heard sometimes on the second floor where the nursery was located. Few have heard these ghostly babies, however, because the second floor is off-limits to visitors. It is reached by claustrophobically narrow stairs, hidden in the walls, because Jefferson thought that grand, open staircases were a waste of space and so did not provide them in his plans.

An older, more somber version of Jefferson's spirit is thought to appear on rare occasions in Monticello's entrance hall, where the Sage of Monticello would welcome important guests. This room is decorated with portraits of historic figures whom Jefferson admired. He hung his own picture among those of his heroes; some claim that in his portrait Jefferson's eyes move and focus on any famous person who tours his home. Supposedly, Jefferson's shade appears in this entrance hall, carefully examining the Native American artifacts that decorate the walls. These handicrafts and works of art were sent to Jefferson by the famous explorers Meriwether Lewis and William Clark, whose monumental expedition had been commissioned by the president. The Native American pieces were obtained in the traditional exchange of gifts accompanying the signing of treaties.

A different aspect of Jefferson's personality is embodied in the ghostly image said to manifest in the great man's own bedroom suite. While Jefferson clearly enjoyed entertaining visitors to his home, he also valued his time alone. His private suite of rooms included his bedroom, a solarium, and a "cabinet," a combination library, office, and sitting room. He had 6,700 books at Monticello, many in Greek or Latin. Within the suite of interconnected rooms, he enjoyed solitude for reading, writing, and undisturbed thinking. This very private environment is thought to be haunted by the hazy, faintly shimmering spirit of Jefferson, seated at his desk, wearing his reading glasses. He occupies a swivel chair of his own invention. Phantoms of his beloved mockingbirds flutter about in large cages nearby.

Some of Monticello's staff who are willing to admit anonymously to having glimpsed the phantom of the great man allege that his spirit can be seen frowning over his plantation account books. The deep frown certainly would be consistent with the living man, for Jefferson dealt with money troubles all of his adult life. Although Jefferson was rich in land, he was usually short of cash. His father-in-law, John Wayles, died deeply in debt, part of which Jefferson had to assume. During the Revolution, British general Lord Charles Cornwallis literally went out of his way to pillage Jefferson's plantation, burning crops and slaughtering animals. Jefferson was proud of leaving public service poorer than when he entered it. His expenses incurred as envoy to Paris were reimbursed with worthless paper currency afterward. While in the White House, he used his own funds to supplement an official entertainment budget he felt to be woefully inadequate. He never really learned to manage his own money, lived with debt all his life, spent lavishly on books and wine, and died bankrupt. His personal experiences with overhanging debt gave him a negative view on public debt. "I sincerely believe," he wrote, "that banking establishments are more dangerous than standing armies, and that the principle of spending to be paid by prosperity, under the name of funding, is but swindling futurity on a large scale."

Perhaps Jefferson's long and unsuccessful struggle to manage his money helps to explain the man's strongly conflicting attitudes and policies concerning slavery. All his life, Jefferson publicly advocated abolition of the evil institution; in the meantime, he owned about two hundred slaves, fifteen of whom worked in his home. In his lifetime, he freed only seven slaves; six of whom are believed by some experts to be his own children, born to his slave Sally Hemings. The seventh freed slave was Sally's brother, James, which brings us to another ghost story.

Allegedly yet another manifestation of Jefferson's spirit appears at Poplar Forest, and this time, Jefferson's shade is in company with the spirit of Sally Hemings. Poplar Forest was Jefferson's vacation retreat, a private hideaway located about ninety miles southwest of Monticello. Like Monticello, Poplar Forest was designed by Jefferson himself, reflecting a lifetime passion for architecture. He began visiting Poplar Forest in 1809, at the age of sixty-six. His visits lasted for between two and four weeks at a time.

Poplar Forest fulfilled Jefferson's need for privacy, something that was increasingly rare at Monticello. A seemingly endless parade of visitors called at Monticello, all eager to meet the greatest surviving leader of the Revolution and, incidentally, enjoy his vastly renowned hospitality. The drain on his household resources and his time were considerable. Ever eager to meet interesting people and enjoy stimulating conversations, Jefferson nonetheless desired peace and quiet with his surviving daughter, Martha, and his twelve grandchildren. Relatively remote and surrounded by 4,812 acres of private land, much of it heavily forested, Poplar Forest was literally a hideaway. Few people outside the family even knew about Poplar Forest in Jefferson's lifetime; its relationship to the third president was almost forgotten until a group of patriots formed a nonprofit foundation to rescue the house from oblivion in 1983.

The unique architecture of Poplar Forest contributes to the romantic mystery of its alleged ghosts. The outer walls form a large octagon, one of Jefferson's favorite geometrical shapes.

The center room is square, some twenty feet on each side, and lit by a sixteen-foot-long skylight. The rooms surrounding this central room are partial octagons.

This central room, lit at night by moonlight and flickering spectral candles, is the scene of the appearance of the slightly phosphorescent forms of Jefferson and Sally Hemings. The two ghosts are said to be seated near one another in a relaxed and tranquil domestic scene of intimacy. Sally's story is as surprising and controversial today as it was during her lifetime.

Sally, whose given name was Sarah, was born to a slave whose own father was an English sea captain. Sally's father is believed to be John Wayles, Jefferson's own father-in-law. She was described by another one of Jefferson's slaves as "mighty near white, very handsome, with long, straight hair."

Jefferson's political enemies accused him of keeping Sally as a concubine. Jefferson made no comment on this, because it was his policy never to offer any public response to personal attacks. Recent DNA tests show that a male in the Jefferson line was the father of Sally's six children. Additional evidence suggests that Thomas Jefferson himself is the father.

It is thought that a relationship between Jefferson and Sally began in Paris in 1787. Jefferson was on a diplomatic mission to France. Sally, then aged fourteen, was brought to France as a companion-servant to Thomas's nine-year-old daughter, Mary. Sally's brother James also came to Paris as a cook and coach-man. Soon after his arrival, James told Jefferson that they needed to discuss his salary. James had learned that France had outlawed slavery; as long as Sally and he were in France, they were free. James was willing to stay with Jefferson, working for payment. The record shows that James and Sally each received salaries while in France.

When Jefferson returned to America, James stayed behind in Paris. Why did Sally, who must have known she would be returning into slavery, go back with him? Neither Jefferson nor Sally wrote any thoughts on their relationship, so we don't know for certain how they saw it. Following Jefferson's death, his daughter Martha gave Sally "her time," a kind of informal freedom. This may have been because Jefferson's huge debts would have prevented his heirs from disposing of property against which his lenders had liens. It is known that three of Sally's children "lived in white society," that is, they passed for white and were genetically seven-eighths white.

Did Jefferson maintain Poplar Forest to live more openly with his "second family?" We'll never know for sure, but the phantoms of Thomas and Sally there seem to illustrate the depth of their relationship.

# James Madison

## 1751–1836
## 4th President, 1809–1817

There must have been times when James Madison thought of himself as "Mr. Dolley Madison," so extravagantly admired was his glamorous wife. Extremely popular first ladies are not just a modern phenomenon, as when John F. Kennedy wryly introduced himself to a French audience as "the man who accompanied Jackie Kennedy to Paris."

Dolley Madison was the first presidential spouse to become a national figure in her own right. She became an American icon of gracious hospitality and vivacious glamour. No wonder Dolley's ghost is far more widely known than that of her husband.

Dolley's ghost is among the most prominent of the many White House spirits. Her shade also appears in the nearby Octagon House and at Montpelier, the Madisons' Virginia plantation.

As president, Madison had a tough act to follow. His good friend and personal hero, Thomas Jefferson, was such a towering figure that Madison's key role in writing the Constitution and his very real accomplishments as president seem to be overshadowed by his predecessor. Sadly, Madison's ghost at Montpelier is the image of an anxious, rather despondent old man, in contrast to the far livelier phantom of Dolley.

Dolley Payne Todd Madison did not have an easy life. Her father, John Payne, once fairly wealthy, had descended into near-poverty as a result of a noble decision to free his slaves. At the time, the colonial government imposed a heavy fine on the former owner for each slave freed. Payne paid his fine and died, leaving his widow, Mary, poor indeed. To pay the bills, she opened a boardinghouse in Philadelphia. Dolley married a local lawyer and bore him two children before he died suddenly, leaving her even poorer than her mother. Dolley moved in with Mary and helped run the boardinghouse. One of the boarders, in town for the Continental Congress, was Thomas Jefferson. Many notable patriots stopped in to talk with Jefferson, including a middle-aged bachelor and lawyer, James Madison. Dolley asked Aaron Burr, military hero and a future vice president, to introduce her to Madison, whom she married in 1794; James was seventeen years older than his new wife.

It should not be a surprise that Dolley's ghost has shown up at the White House, as she holds a record that will never be broken. Dolley served as widower Thomas Jefferson's official hostess for eight years and continued to direct White House hospitality during her husband's two terms. During her sixteen years of association with the White House, Dolley took an active interest in beautifying both the house and its grounds.

It was Dolley, for instance, who ordered the now-famous rose garden to be planted, a spot she really loved. Another first lady, Mrs. Woodrow Wilson, learned the extent of Dolley's affection for the rose garden a century later. Edith Wilson wanted to move it and ordered workmen to dig up the bushes. When they showed up, spades in hand, they were stopped by a dainty woman who wore frilly old-fashioned clothing and a turban on her head. There are two versions of the story. In one, the petite lady simply stood by the rose bushes, admiring the blooms and smelling their sweet scent. She refused to move out of the way to allow the transplant work to begin.

In another version of the story, Dolley's ghost gave the workers a good tongue-lashing and scared them off. When the frustrated workers explained to Mrs. Wilson why her orders hadn't been carried out, the first lady was amazed at their description of the turbaned figure. Dolley became famous for her feathered turbans, which she wore because they added height, making her less self-conscious about her short stature. (She was a good match for Madison, our shortest president, who stood 5 foot, 4 inches.) Mrs. Wilson showed the men a picture of Dolley and asked them if she was the lady who didn't want the roses moved. Yes, agreed the workmen. No one since then has attempted to move the rose garden.

Dolley's ghost, turban and all, is said to also haunt the Octagon House, a historic building only a block from the White House. Dolley saved the Gilbert Stuart portrait of George Washington from destruction when British troops burned the White House on August 24, 1814. Dolley fled the advancing troops, carrying the portrait and some important documents to safety. Only the sandstone walls of the White House remained, leaving the Madisons homeless. The wealthy owners of the Octagon House allowed the president and Dolley to use their house as a temporary executive residence.

Octagon House, built in 1801, had survived the burning of Washington because its owners lent it to the French ambassador, who flew the French flag over the house. This spared the structure for its historic role as a substitute White House and as the site of Dolley's ghostly appearances.

The diminutive, elegant figure glides through the rooms of the Octagon House. A whiff of lilac perfume, Dolley's favorite, follows along with the graciously smiling phantom. She nods to the right and left as she progresses, the epitome of hospitality. Dolley well understood the political value of invitations to the executive mansion. She made it a point to call on the wives of newly arrived senators and congressmen. Invitations to Dolley's weekly "drawing rooms" for tea and cookies were hot tickets for Washington's social and political leaders.

When Dolley lived in Philadelphia, she often visited Haddonfield, New Jersey, where her uncle, Hugh Creighton, ran the Indian King Tavern. Dolley had been reared a Quaker, which at the time meant she wasn't supposed to dance. Vivacious Dolley is said to have watched the dances held on the Indian King's second floor, however, tapping her toes and enjoying the lively scene. The Indian King Tavern, which still stands on Haddonfield's King's Highway, is said to host Dolley's happily smiling ghost. Party-loving, rather flamboyant Dolley must have felt restrained by the Quakers' strict rules. Perhaps she wasn't too disappointed when they excommunicated her for marrying Episcopalian James Madison.

Dolley should not be thought of as just a fun-loving social butterfly; indeed, she was a worker bee, gathering the honey of political goodwill for her husband. Even after the Madisons left the White House, she remained at the pinnacle of political and social life. All of her life, Dolley remained opposed to slavery, which must have led to some uncomfortable social moments in Virginia's plantation society, but her personal charm always prevailed.

When James and Dolley retired from public life to live at Montpelier, James was sixty-five and Dolley was forty-eight. Dolley's spirit is said to favor the temple, a classical-style gazebo on the grounds of the estate. The temple was a favorite summer retreat, built atop an ice well. The ice well was a deep pit in which ice cut from ponds in the winter was stored. The ice stockpiled under the temple made it a little cooler than the main house and also provided ice for cool drinks and ice cream. There is Dolley's phantom, enjoying the cool temple, sipping on a cold drink or digging into a bowl of her famous peach ice cream.

When Dolley died at Montpelier at age eighty-one, President Zachary Taylor led a large delegation of legislators and officials to attend her funeral. Dolley would have been pleased at the turnout to her last public function. Some guests at the post-funeral luncheon in Montpelier swore that they briefly glimpsed Dolley's sweetly smiling face in the entrance hall, as though welcoming the mourners.

James Madison's spirit, in contrast, can best be described as dispirited. For a variety of reasons, Madison's old age was not a happy time. Just like his good friend and neighbor Thomas Jefferson, Madison discovered that his plantation was not very profitable. And, like Jefferson, Madison felt obligated to entertain hordes of visitors and well-wishers. Dolley was renowned for her lavish dinner parties. She did not subscribe to the European elite's pattern of a few choice morsels served in a fancy sauce. Dolley served up generous portions of good plain American cooking, more like a "harvest home" supper, smirked a European diplomat. Dolley personified southern hospitality—a hospitality the Madisons could not afford.

Madison had no biological children. Dolley had two sons by her first husband; one of them died just before her marriage to James. Her surviving son, John Todd, turned out to be an alcoholic, a degenerate gambler, a shameless womanizer, and a thief. Madison personally covered more than $40,000 of John's debts, a staggering sum at the time.

Harassed by creditors and deeply saddened by John Todd's behavior, Madison arranged for Congress to buy his priceless political papers on his death, hoping to provide for his widow in her old age. Madison brooded over his papers, constantly reviewing them. Physically ill and possibly mentally ill as well, he began to literally rewrite history. He not only edited his own writings to embellish his role in history, but even attempted to imitate Jefferson's handwriting, adding comments that Jefferson never made, at least in writing. Now, Madison's ghost sits in his library, poring over documents, pathetically reliving his glory days and trying to polish his reputation—a reputation that would shine brightly on its own without enhancement efforts by the frustrated and embittered old man.

There are those who claim to have witnessed Madison's ghost, visibly angry, at Montpelier whenever political events upset his spirit. Madison was a strong advocate of the checks-and-balances philosophy that he wrote into the Constitution. No one branch—executive, legislative, or judicial—should have unrestrained power over the other. If it is true that any imbalances developing call forth the shade of James Madison, his might be among America's busiest ghosts, and its angriest as well.

# James Monroe

## 1758–1831
## 5th President, 1817–1825

The ghost, like the once-living man, is an imposing figure—six feet tall and of muscular build. Intelligence seems to shine from his eyes as the phantom surveys his surroundings. At first, it seems as though the spirit is trapped inside an elaborate cage, a gothic scrollwork of iron. But the wispy ghost passes through the ironwork as though it were not there—ghosts are not restricted by material barriers. The lacy iron that surrounds and protects the tomb was erected in 1865 by the state of Virginia to honor one of its most famous sons, James Monroe.

Monroe's ghost is not particularly notable, rather like the man himself. While his major contribution to American history, his proclamation of the so-called Monroe Doctrine, is widely known, Monroe's rather self-effacing personality has led to his being overshadowed by more dramatic and assertive presidents. His ghost at Hollywood Cemetery in Richmond, Virginia, seems to be quietly reflective, so unlike the heroic vision of George Washington leading troops into battle at Gettysburg, for example. Monroe's phantom, at least as reported by some, thoughtfully rubs his left shoulder as though massaging an old wound. Monroe is the only American president to have been seriously wounded in battle during the Revolution. Major James Monroe fought under General Washington at the Battle of Trenton. In Emanuel Leutze's famous painting *Washington Crossing the Delaware*, Monroe is the one holding the flag. It took him three months to recover, and he carried that British bullet in him for the rest of his life.

Monroe, like so many presidents, was a bundle of paradoxes. In his day, he was enormously popular. In his reelection in 1820, he received 231 out of 232 Electoral College votes. He was not a charismatic or inspirational leader, but rather a methodical and efficient bureaucrat. His ghost, reportedly, is calm and undramatic—so was the man. One of his biographers observed that Monroe's "virtue was not in flying high but in walking orderly, his talents were exercised not in grandeur but in mediocrity."

On the other hand, Monroe was famously honest, a noble trait that was unfortunately not universal among presidents. His friend Jefferson said, "Monroe was so honest that if you turned his soul inside out there would not be a spot on it."

By old age, he was financially broke. He had not been born rich; his father was a carpenter and farmer. But he had married the daughter of a wealthy New York family, and she brought her extravagant tastes along with her money. When Monroe served as American Ambassador to France, his wife Elizabeth bought an entire house full of fancy French furniture for their Virginia home. She and his two daughters, Eliza and Maria, spent money much faster than Monroe could make it.

In his impoverished old age, Monroe went to New York to live with his younger daughter, Maria, who had married into a rich family, the Gouverneurs. And so it came to be that Monroe was buried in the Gouverneur family vault in Manhattan's Marble Cemetery. Monroe died on July 4, 1831. Exactly twenty-seven years later he was reburied in Hollywood Cemetery. Apparently, Monroe's ghost was confused when the body was moved from his first burial place to Richmond. His ghost, it is said, hung around the Marble Cemetery in Lower Manhattan for a while, until it too migrated to Richmond.

There have been no reported ghostly appearances of Monroe's first lady, but the phantoms of his two daughters are alleged to have shown up in the White House and in the nearby Stephen Decatur House. Both manifestations were onetime appearances, apparently.

Eliza earned a reputation as a bossy, self-centered, and somewhat vindictive hostess during the eight years she functioned as her father's official White House social director. Her sickly mother turned over her official duties to Eliza, who ruled with an unforgiving iron hand. Those who crossed Eliza would never get a White House invitation, regardless of their importance. Eliza ran her sister's wedding, the first ever in the White House, as a very exclusive affair, with only thirty-two guests. Uninvited politicians and diplomats were outraged. Decades later Eliza's ghost is said to have shown up during James Buchanan's term, abrasively ordering servants about as they prepared the East Room for an important reception. Allegedly, the phantom was rude and disruptive, attempting to rearrange the place cards on the tables. The ghost evaporated like fog in sunlight when the head butler showed up to see what the fuss was about.

The spirit of Monroe's younger daughter, Maria, was reported once at the Decatur House, which still stands on Lafayette Square opposite the White House. Her shade was said to look very distraught, as well it might be. The Decatur House was the scene of a nightmarish end to a grand party in honor of newly-weds Maria and Samuel Gouverneur. So many people had been snubbed by Eliza's insistence on the very short invitation list for Maria's wedding that the couple wanted to hold a more inclusive reception to soothe hurt feelings. War of 1812 naval hero Stephen Decatur offered to host the party. Unwisely, Decatur accepted a challenge to a duel, in which he was seriously wounded. The party atmosphere ended abruptly when the mortally wounded host, dying in great pain, was brought home. Maria's sole reported appearance as a ghost at Decatur House is supposed to have materialized on the one hundredth anniversary of Decatur's death on March 20, 1920. Will either sister ever show up again? Only time will tell.

# John Quincy Adams

## 1767–1848
## 6th President, 1825–1829

One of the first appearances of the infamous Demon Cat in the United States Capitol may have been to foretell the death of John Quincy Adams. The ghost of Adams has in good time joined the Demon Cat as one of many spirits roaming the labyrinthine halls of the stately capitol.

The Demon Cat, or D.C., as it is nicknamed, is said to appear in the crypt under the Capitol to warn of impending disaster or death. Its more recent sightings are supposed to have occurred shortly before the 1929 stock market crash, John F. Kennedy's assassination, and 9/11.

Those who have seen D.C. agree that it first appears to be a cuddly little kitten, coal black and eager to be petted. Then, quickly, before the observer's horrified eyes, D.C. grows into a large, aggressive tomcat, all fangs and claws, its yellow eyes brimming with evil. Panic sets in, and as the terrified witness turns to flee, D.C. disappears.

D.C.'s choice of the crypt for its Capitol appearances is significant. The crypt was intended to receive the body of George Washington, so that in a sense, the whole Capitol would be his monument. Washington, however, left instructions that he was to be buried on the grounds of his beloved Mount Vernon, and so his Capitol crypt never was occupied, except by D.C.

D.C. also has been reported in the basement of the White House. That it materialized in the Capitol to foretell Adams's death rather than in the White House accurately reflects Adams's political career. His one term as president probably was not the highlight of his life as far as he was concerned. Many historians agree. It is notable that the president's ghost haunts several locations within the Capitol and not the White House.

Adams entered the White House on March 4, 1825, under a cloud of distrust and disrespect. In the hotly contested election of 1824, four major candidates sought the presidency. None achieved a clear majority but Andrew Jackson earned a plurality of both the popular and Electoral College votes. It was up to the House of Representatives to choose the winner. Adams cut a deal with Henry Clay, who came in third in popular votes and happened to be speaker of the House. Clay supported Adams, who as president made Clay secretary of state. Jackson and his many supporters never forgave Adams. After Jackson resoundingly defeated Adams in the 1828 election, Adams refused to attend Jackson's inauguration and returned home to Massachusetts. His home state then sent him back to Washington for eight consecutive terms in the House of Representatives. No doubt Congressman Adams was much happier than President Adams. On February 21, 1848, John Quincy Adams collapsed on the floor of the House. He was carried to the nearby Speaker's Room, where he died two days later.

The phantom of Adams haunts the Speaker's Room. The bald high-domed head is fringed with long, wispy white hair. The almost-transparent ghost has a stern, no-nonsense expression that frequently becomes a deep frown. This is anything but a lighthearted spirit, for Adams was a serious man with a serious quest. All his life, he was a determined foe of slavery. He foresaw that a great civil war might be necessary to finally abolish human slavery. He said, "Though it cost the blood of millions of white men, let it come. Let justice be done, though the heavens fall." Adams was the only president who knew both the nation's Founding Fathers and Abraham Lincoln, with whom he served in the House during Lincoln's term in Congress.

In addition to the Speaker's Room, the ghost of Adams is said to haunt the old Supreme Court chamber in the Capitol and for good reason. A lawyer by trade and a passionate abolitionist by heart, Adams defended fifty-three Africans in the famous 1841

*Amistad* case. The *Amistad* was a Spanish ship transporting slaves from Africa, bound for Cuba. In mid-ocean the slaves revolted, killed the ship's officers, and then sailed to an American port. The government intended to send the Africans to Cuba to be tried for murder and enslaved if not executed. The Africans wanted to go back to Africa. Antislavery groups asked Adams to argue for the defense. The nine Supreme Court justices included five southerners who owned or had owned slaves.

Adams won the case; he never submitted a bill for his services. It was a great triumph for the man, and his ghost often can be seen in the onetime courtroom. The phantom paces the floor as it makes its silent argument. This ghost is not distracted by the living. If a person intrudes on its dramatic appeal to the court, the image just slowly fades into oblivion.

Some claim to have spotted Adams's ghost at his burial place in the crypt he shares with his father, mother, and wife at United First Parish Church in Quincy, Massachusetts. That particular venue, however, does not seem to host his spirit as frequently as the two locations in the U.S. Capitol that represent the distinguished man's proudest accomplishments.

# Andrew Jackson

## 1767–1845
## 7th President, 1829–1837

Andrew Jackson led a colorful life. His ghost has become one of the most famous spectral inhabitants of the White House, and many claim to have glimpsed his shade in several other locations as well.

The term "charisma" wasn't used in the early nineteenth century, but Jackson had plenty of it. The men who followed him into battle at New Orleans gave him the nickname Old Hickory, because they thought him to be as tough as that type of hard wood.

Jackson was a natural leader. Men followed him with loyal enthusiasm into battles of both the military and political varieties. Apparently, few people were neutral about Jackson. He was loved or hated with equal depth of passion. A redhead like Washington and Jefferson, Jackson had a fiery temper. Like Washington, Jackson could curse with the best of them. In the heat of battle, he displayed an extensive and inventive vocabulary of profanity. His mastery of invective was put to frequent use when he was frustrated by political opponents. Perhaps this is why his ghost in the White House is heard more often than it is seen.

Several first ladies and many White House staffers over the years believed they heard Jackson's ghost stomping about and swearing in his onetime bedroom on the second floor. This room was known as the Rose Room until it was renamed the Queen's Bedroom in honor of its occupancy by England's Queen Elizabeth II on her several visits to the White House. There is no record of any supernatural experiences there on the part of the queen. Perhaps Jackson's ghost would be like the living man in being careful not to curse in the presence of ladies. Jackson was a widower when president, which may explain his free use of naughty words when alone in his bedroom.

The statue of Jackson in Lafayette Square across from the White House is said to be haunted. Late at night, according to some, the statue seems to come alive. Jackson appears to be massaging various old wounds, of which he had many.

Old Hickory was the last American president to have actively participated in the Revolutionary War. He enlisted as a courier at the age of thirteen and was in constant danger as he ran along the front lines with orders and messages. At the Battle of Hanging Rock, fourteen-year-old Andy was captured by the British. An officer apparently ordered Andy to kneel and clean his boots. Jackson refused, making several undiplomatic comments about the officer's character and ancestry. Angered, the officer struck out at the boy with his saber, giving Jackson a nasty gash in his scalp and cutting his upraised fist to the bone. It is said that Jackson wore his hair long to conceal the livid scar, and that his left hand throbbed with pain in damp weather.

The statue has been seen rubbing its left chest and left arm, where Jackson received other wounds. In 1806, Jackson challenged Charles Dickinson, widely believed to be the best shot in Tennessee, to a duel. Dickinson had slandered Jackson's wife Rachel, and he became furious. Dickinson fired first, hitting Jackson in the chest, shattering two ribs and just missing the heart. Jackson shot back and killed Dickinson before collapsing. Jackson carried the bullet in him for the rest of his life. Then in 1813, Jackson was involved in a gunfight with two thugs, the Benton brothers. A pistol ball lodged in his left arm and eventually was removed by a White House doctor in 1832.

The ghost of Jackson is said to haunt the Taylor Cabin in Jonesboro, Tennessee. Chris Taylor built the cabin in 1777 and ran a kind of frontier boardinghouse at which the twenty-one-year-old Jackson stayed at least briefly. Jackson's ghost is believed to walk about the cabin, exit by the back door, and return to enter by the front door.

Jackson's strong devotion to his wife, Rachel, was well-documented during his lifetime. Jackson's spirit continues to display his undying love for his soul mate, as evidenced by the ghost's alleged behavior at the Hermitage, Jackson's home near Nashville.

For all Jackson's reputation as a hard man, he had a tender romantic side and was deeply in love with Rachel. Andrew met Rachel when he stayed at a boardinghouse run by Rachel's mother. At the time, Rachel was separated from her abusive first husband, Lewis Robards, who claimed he would file for divorce and then leave the territory. So Andrew and Rachel got married. Years later, however, when Jackson had risen to national fame, Robards tried to blackmail the Jacksons, asserting that Rachel had committed bigamy. Rachel had to divorce him and remarry Jackson, whose political enemies labeled his wife as a loose woman, which she definitely was not.

Jackson figured that, by entering politics, he had opened himself to all manner of criticism and character assassination, but was furious at attacks on Rachel. A month after his victory in the rancorous election of 1828, Rachel died of a heart attack. Jackson was overwhelmed with grief. He buried her in the flower garden she planted and visited her grave every day while in residence at the Hermitage. While in the White House, Jackson read every evening from Rachel's prayer book while holding a miniature portrait of her in his hand. He had erected over her grave a small, Greek-style temple and was buried beside her in June 1845, seventeen years after her untimely death. Jackson always believed that Rachel's fatal heart attack was caused by the stress of the vicious gossip directed at her during the political campaign. His White House sessions with her prayer book and portrait may have been private séances in which he communed with her soul.

In January 1835, two years before Jackson left office, an unemployed house painter named Richard Lawrence attempted to shoot the president as he left the Capitol. Lawrence's gun misfired, so he drew a second pistol and aimed, but that weapon also misfired. Rachel is said to have come to Andrew in a dream that night, saying that this miraculous escape from death meant that Jackson was a man of destiny and would be remembered as one of America's great presidents. This further deepened Jackson's belief that he and Rachel had a mystic bond that transcended death itself.

Some people report that Andrew and Rachel Jackson's spirits still appear in the Hermitage and at the little temple that marks their graves. The couple is described as being like wisps of fog or even almost transparent. They are so focused on one another that they pay no attention to the living. The phantom lovers are said to hold hands and kiss just before fading from view.

Jackson had other brushes with the supernatural. Shortly after his famous victory at New Orleans, he became interested in the story of the Bell Witch. This malevolent spirit, who harassed John Bell and his family in the early 1800s, is one of America's best-known and best-documented hauntings. The Bell family had a farm near Nashville. A phantom identifying herself as "Kate" sometimes appeared as a cat, vulture, or dog, attacking Bell's family by punching, scratching, and biting them in the night.

Jackson heard about the witch and decided to confront her. With military precision, he hired a "witch layer," or ghost hunter, to accompany him and his good friend Sam Houston, who had fought under Jackson at New Orleans. According to the story, as Jackson's carriage turned onto Bell's farm, the wheels seemed to be frozen to the ground. Nothing could budge it. A deep voice issued from a nearby bush, "I'll see you tonight, General!" Jackson got no sleep that night, as unseen teeth and nails left him a bloody and bruised man. He departed in defeat, saying he'd rather fight the British than the Bell Witch.

Incidentally, the Bell Witch is supposed to have persisted in her torments for more than a century. According to some, she still haunts a nearby cave, the Bell's Witch Cavern.

In contrast to forming half of an obviously devoted couple, the supposed ghost of Rachel Jackson is said to haunt the

Tennessee State Capitol. Her shade is believed to appear most often in the tower of the building. Since the Capitol was not completed until after Rachel's death, she could not have been familiar with the building in life. It is not clear why Rachel's spirit would visit the state capitol, but perhaps ghosts need not follow any rules. So far, Rachel's ghost does not seem to have caused any harm or wreaked any mischief on the politicians there, which might be testimony to her strong religious principles. The vicious gossip directed at her by partisans of the opposing political party certainly wounded her husband. Rachel's epitaph reads, "A being so gentle and so virtuous slander might wound, but could not dishonor." And so, if Rachel's spirit haunts the Capitol, it is consistent with the living lady that she evidentially bears an ill will towards partisan politics.

A seldom seen but most interesting ghost at the Hermitage is that of Lincoya, the Jacksons' adopted Native American son. The orphaned infant was found on the battlefield at Tallushatchee in 1813, where Jackson had just defeated a faction of Creek Indians known as the Redsticks. When soldiers brought the tiny boy to Jackson, he immediately decided to adopt him. Lincoya was raised at the Hermitage as Jackson's son, sadly dying of tuberculosis just five months before Jackson won the presidency. It is claimed that Lincoya's apparition appears as an energetic and playful boy of eight or ten, running across the lawn at the Hermitage.

# Martin Van Buren

## 1782–1862
## 8th President, 1837–1841

In her fascinating compendium, *The Encyclopedia of Ghosts and Spirits*, renowned author Rosemary Ellen Guiley reminds us, "Contrary to popular belief, most ghosts are not seen in graveyards but in structures—houses and buildings." The ghost of Martin Van Buren unsurprisingly chooses to manifest not in a cold and lonely crypt, but in the gracious home in which he spent, by his own account, the happiest years of his life. Van Buren lived at Lindenwald, his estate near his birthplace at Kinderhook, New York, for the twenty-one years after he left the White House. While his places of birth and death were only a few miles apart, Van Buren had traveled a huge distance in fame and fortune.

The spirit of Van Buren, interestingly enough, often materializes in the company of his favorite son, John. The phantoms of father and son appear at the dining table in Lindenwald, relaxed and sociable, doing what they did best—charming their company and enjoying fine food and drink. Some observers report that the phantom of the former president can be seen surreptitiously reaching under his waistcoat to loosen the corset he wore in old age to hide an expanding belly. In youth, he was five foot, six inches tall and had a slim build, but in middle age his fondness for fancy wines imported from France, Italy, and Germany, accompanied by generous servings of gourmet food, had expanded his gut.

The wealthy connoisseur of fine living and owner of a beautiful mansion and more than two hundred acres of prime farmland had come a long way from the son of a Dutch tavern keeper. Martin was reared in a Dutch-speaking household.

English was his second language, but he used it skillfully and persuasively, becoming a successful lawyer before entering politics full time. The red-headed Van Buren quickly earned a reputation as the consummate politician, quietly wheeling and dealing to achieve his goals, and was nicknamed the "Red Fox" and the "Little Magician." Perhaps that explains the watchful, self-satisfied faint smile on the lips of his ghost.

When Van Buren was only thirty-six years old, he lost his wife of twelve years. Overcome with grief, he placed his four sons in the care of relatives and became a workaholic. After eight years in the state legislature, he was elected governor of New York but resigned to become Andrew Jackson's secretary of state and then vice president. With Jackson's strong support, he was elected president in 1836. As he said later, the two happiest days of his life were entering the presidency and leaving it. The financial panic of 1837 wrecked the economy and Van Buren got the blame. In the campaign of 1840, the Red Fox got a new nickname—"Van Ruin." He was happy to retire to the life of a country gentleman.

The second half of the ghostly duo at Lindenwald is the spirit of John Van Buren, Martin's second son and his favorite. John was like a distorted mirror image of his father. Martin was a great lawyer; John was even more brilliant. Martin, who had tended bar in his father's tavern as a young man, had a tremendous appetite and capacity for whiskey but was never drunk; John was a raging alcoholic. Martin appreciated female society but avoided scandal; John was a notorious womanizer and degenerate gambler.

So there they sit, side by side, father and son, in ghostly form in Lindenwald's dining room. Martin Van Buren's spirit is a monument to hard work, shrewd planning, a touch of luck, and skillful skirting of scandal. His son's shade reflects the consequences of self-indulgence carried to extremes. The Little Magician's political prowess carried him to the White House for one unhappy term, but his favorite son turned out to be a sad magnification of his father's character flaws.

# William Henry Harrison

## 1773–1841
## 9th President, 1841

Among presidents, it is more typical than not that their public image and actual history and character are not the same. In the presidential campaign of 1840, William Henry Harrison was portrayed as the "Log Cabin and Hard Cider" candidate. Originally intended as a slur by the opposition, this slogan was adopted gleefully by the Harrison campaign as a positive image to emphasize the contrast with incumbent Martin Van Buren, who was portrayed as drinking tea from English china cups. In reality, Harrison had little to do with either log cabins or hard cider, but one of his two reported ghostly appearances is said to reflect popular perceptions of the ninth president. When people see, or think they see, a ghost, is their perception shaped more by what they expect to see than by a more accurate supernatural manifestation of the deceased?

There are two ghost stories about Harrison. The more widely known has his spirit, heard but not seen, rummaging about in the attic of the White House. This particular apparition hasn't been heard from in a long time, probably because the White House no longer has an attic. The attic was converted into a third floor of private living space back in 1927. Why was Harrison's ghost up in the attic in the first place? Perhaps he was looking for something his wife had packed back in Ohio but wasn't available to unpack. Anna Harrison hadn't arrived yet at the White House before her husband died there.

Harrison was, until the election of Ronald Reagan, the oldest man ever to occupy the White House. He still holds the record for the shortest presidency—thirty-two days before dying of pneumonia contracted during a lengthy inaugural address in a freezing rain.

The other supposed appearance of Harrison's spirit is said to occur on occasion at his tomb. It is this ghost that seems at odds with the habits of the once-living man. The log cabin and hard cider image notwithstanding, Harrison wasn't familiar with log cabins. He had been born into a prosperous and influential Virginia family—his father signed the Declaration of Independence and owned slaves (William himself, though, was strongly anti-slavery).

Harrison joined the army at age eighteen and achieved fame as an Indian fighter at the Battle of Tippecanoe. He served in the Ohio legislature and then in Congress as a representative and a senator. He also was ambassador to Colombia, where he got to know the great liberator of South America, Simón Bolívar. At one point, Harrison registered for classes at the University of Pennsylvania's prestigious medical school, but he did not complete his studies.

In private, Harrison probably had little to do with hard cider. Although he did operate a whiskey distillery on his old farm to use some of his corn crop, he drank very sparingly if at all. Some say he was a teetotaler. Still, he knew a good public relations ploy when he saw one and began toting about a jug of hard cider in public appearances.

Harrison's ghost, the story goes, occasionally haunts his tomb, which stands atop a hill overlooking the Ohio River at North Bend, west of Cincinnati. This phantom is said to appear near sunset, seated and gazing out at the lovely view. The spirit, wracked by evidently painful spasms of coughing, pauses often to sip from a large jug of hard cider. Can drinking hard cider cure a cold? Evidently not.

# John Tyler

## 1790–1862
## 10th President, 1841–1845

Not a particularly famous Chief Executive, John Tyler is most notable for being the first vice president to be promoted to the presidency after the death of his predecessor. Tyler's presidency was not a very successful one. He is most remembered as the president who fathered the most children; at fifteen, the record is most likely to stand.

Tyler's ghost is listed among the many that haunt the White House, but his spirit there is not nearly as famous, or frequently seen, as those of Dolley Madison, Andrew Jackson, or Abraham Lincoln. The much better known supernatural events connected with Tyler are the ghost that allegedly haunts his plantation home and the "crisis apparition," which appeared to his wife, Julia.

The supernormal appearance of a dead or living person too distant to be a normal perception is an apparition. As Rosemary Ellen Guiley observed in her *Encyclopedia of Ghosts and Spirits*, "Contrary to popular belief, the majority of cases on record concern apparitions of the living and not of the dead." Public opinion surveys, as reported by Guiley, suggest that at least ten percent of the population report apparitions, of which two-thirds involved a living person.

Crisis apparitions are those that appear during times of trauma or great danger to the person who appears in an apparition. These events involve very close emotional ties, as between husband and wife or parent and child. A crisis apparition warned Julia Tyler of her husband's impending death.

Tyler's first wife, Letitia, died in the White House. He met his second wife, Julia, literally by accident. Julia and her father were among the guests on a ceremonial first cruise of a brand new warship, the U.S.S. *Princeton*. A demonstration of her powerful guns was planned to impress President Tyler. A gun blew up, killing the secretary of war and Julia's dad. Tyler personally rescued Julia and comforted her so well that they were married four months later. Julia bore John seven children, the last when she was forty and he was seventy.

A slaveholder, Tyler supported the Confederacy during the Civil War and was elected to the Confederate House of Representatives. Soon after he went to Richmond to attend his new duties there, Julia had a vivid dream. She saw her husband on his deathbed. On the wooden headboard of the bed in which he lay dying was carved a large eagle, its wings outspread. Julia woke up in a cold sweat. She journeyed up to Richmond to warn her husband that the Angel of Death was hovering over him. Tyler smiled at his wife's anxiety. He felt fine and reassured her. She went home. The next day the former president was dead. When Julia reached the hotel room where his body lay, she saw him in the bed with an eagle on the headboard.

What was the significance of the eagle? Look on the back of a dollar bill. The Great Seal of the United States features an eagle, wings outspread. This eagle is a symbol of the federal government, the union which Tyler, as an elected member of the Confederate government, was about to betray. About to take his office, Tyler was on the brink of treason to the Union he'd served as president. Had he been stricken down by an avenging angel? Julia wondered about that for the rest of her life.

Tyler owned a large plantation in Charles City County, near Williamsburg, Virginia. Its original name was Walnut Grove. Tyler changed the name to Sherwood Forest, because his enemies called him a "Robin Hood," an outlaw politician because he was not a party loyalist. Sherwood Forest is said to be haunted by a ghost who was present there during Tyler's lifetime and who may still be in residence. Tyler himself is said to have sensed "a presence" as he put it. This ghost is called the "Gray Lady," as she usually appears as a misty, gray figure, walking about the halls of Sherwood Forest. She is, the story goes, a middle-aged woman of matronly figure. She calmly goes about her business, which seems to involve an infant, because she often carries baby clothing and diapers, sometimes a baby bottle. One theory has it that the Gray Lady is the spirit of a nursemaid who was employed at the house before Tyler bought the property. She was in charge of an infant who died in a tragic accident. Filled with grief, her spirit has been unable to leave. When dogs encounter the Gray Lady, they run in the opposite direction, whimpering. Cats freeze on the spot, arch their spines, lay back their ears, and hiss.

Many people over the years report glimpsing the Gray Lady. If you would like to try your luck, Sherwood Forest offers public tours, but ghost sightings are not guaranteed.

# James K. Polk

## 1795–1849
## 11th President, 1845–1849

James K. Polk may be the best president you've never heard of. Historians call him the first dark horse candidate. He also could be called the dark horse president, as few but historians are familiar with him, despite some really impressive accomplishments.

Polk's ghost, according to the many who claim to have seen it at the Tennessee State Capitol in Nashville, is very much like the man himself, quietly industrious. Polk and his wife Sarah are buried on the Capitol grounds under a small, Greek-style temple that looks much like a garden gazebo. When Polk's spirit appears here, it is invariably accompanied by that of Sarah. The two phantoms sit at right angles to each other, studying documents that they pass back and forth.

Although Polk might appear on a top ten list of obscure presidents, historians have placed him tenth on a list of the ten most effective chief executives we've ever had. He was a hard-working man who once remarked that a president who had any leisure time wasn't doing his job. His wife said that he wore himself out in the service of his country, and she was right. Polk had the shortest retirement of any former president. Exactly 103 days after leaving the White House, he died of a heart attack.

Polk was buried on the grounds of Polk Place, the home he'd purchased as a retirement residence. His devoted wife kept the house as a memorial to him for forty-two years until she died in 1891 at the age of eighty-eight. Following her death, Polk Place was sold and demolished. James and Sarah's remains were reburied in their present graves at the Capitol.

Polk had never enjoyed robust health. As a teenager, he suffered from kidney stone fragments lodged in the urinary tract, an extremely painful condition. An operation to remove them was botched by a country doctor, rendering Polk sterile.

That Sarah's phantom would appear at her husband's side is perfectly in character. Born in wealth, Sarah was well educated and took an active role in her husband's career, a sort of nineteenth-century Eleanor Roosevelt. She wrote his speeches, and he discussed everything with her. A strict Presbyterian, she banned alcohol and dancing from the White House. Still, she was such a well-informed conversationalist that she was a popular White House hostess who lobbied congressmen and senators to support her husband's policies.

It is said that Polk's ghost frequently holds a large map of North America, which he views with evident satisfaction, and well he should. Polk was a strongly expansionist president. He risked war with Britain over the disputed Oregon Territory before agreeing to the present boundary with Canada. He waged a successful war with Mexico, taking what had been the northern half of that country. He even offered to buy Cuba from Spain, but the Spanish said it wasn't for sale.

JAMES K. POLK

Polk's spirit, unaccompanied by his wife's ghost, is also said to appear at the only remaining Polk house, a two-story home in Nashville built by his father in 1812. His ghost is said to appear at the old cast-iron garden fountain moved there when Polk Place was demolished.

Another venue for his ghost is the Old Chester Inn in Jonesborough. Polk's idol, Andrew Jackson, is also said to haunt this inn. There, Polk's phantom can be seen in earnest conversation with Jackson. Historians called Polk the "Last Jacksonian." Perhaps Polk's spirit is happiest communing with that of his hero.

# Zachary Taylor

## 1784–1850
## 12th President, 1849–1850

Zachary Taylor's ghost is not happy, if indeed it is the shade of the twelfth president. But who else's ghost could it be, hanging about Taylor's tomb in the Zachary Taylor National Cemetery in Louisville, Kentucky?

As far as anyone can remember, Taylor's ghost did not appear until 1991, 141 years after his untimely, and somewhat suspicious, death on July 9, 1850. Not by coincidence, the ghost made himself known to the living after the body was exhumed. The purpose was to solve the mystery surrounding his death.

The official cause of death was listed as acute peritonitis. On July 4, Taylor had officiated at the laying of the foundation of the Washington Monument on the National Mall of the nation's capital. It was a blistering hot and humid day. Returning to the White House, the president, against the advice of his doctor, had consumed a large quantity of cold milk and iced cherries. He had also snacked on presents of food given him by admirers at the dedication ceremonies. Within hours, he was wracked by spasms of severe vomiting and bloody diarrhea. The symptoms worsened. His doctors bled him with no effect. On July 8, he predicted he would die, and on the next day he did.

Some historians speculate that Taylor, not Lincoln, was the first president to be victim of an assassination plot. They believe that Taylor was poisoned. Arsenic poisoning would have produced identical symptoms. At the time of his death, no autopsy had been performed.

On June 17, 1991, with the permission of one of Taylor's descendents, the mausoleum was opened and small tissue and bone samples were removed from the coffin. Lab tests indicated that no abnormal quantities of arsenic could be detected after 141 years. Skeptics distrust the results or believe that strychnine poison was used. But who would poison him and why? The hero of the Mexican War, "Old Rough and Ready," as Taylor was nicknamed, had served in the army for forty years. He had received his lieutenant's commission from his cousin, President James Madison. Taylor was widely popular following his triumphs against Mexico. He received a large majority of votes though he had never held elective office before. He had few enemies. Why assassinate him?

The answer could lie in the rising tensions over the issue of slavery. Taylor owned slaves at his Louisiana plantation; his father had owned slaves. Taylor, however, was opposed to the spread of slavery into the new southwestern lands acquired in the war with Mexico. For one thing, he believed that the drier climate of the southwest could not support cotton, and so slavery as it was known in Dixie could not exist. Southerners may have concluded that Taylor was no friend of the South, despite his personal slave holding and his daughter's marriage to future Confederate President Jefferson Davis.

Was he really poisoned? Critics of the assassination theory point out that Taylor was in poor health before his death. He had contracted yellow fever and malaria early in life and was described by associates as looking pale and tired while in the White House.

Why has his spirit decided to appear at his Louisville mausoleum, and why does the ghost seem to have an angry face? Was Taylor's shade annoyed that his final resting place was disturbed? Or is his spirit surprised and angry to learn of his possible poisoning?

In contrast, a few people have glimpsed Taylor's ghost at the site of his onetime summer home on the Gulf at Pascagoula in Mississippi. This manifestation is distinctly cheerful compared to the mausoleum spirit. This is the relaxed, vacationing version of his persona, which is said to appear near the granite monument marking his summer home, long since demolished.

# Millard Fillmore

## 1800–1874
## 13th President, 1850–1853

Poor Millard Fillmore. The unhappy and undistinguished presidency of the nation's thirteenth chief executive seems to conform to the curse of the number thirteen. He was promoted to the White House by the sudden and suspicious death of his very popular predecessor, Zachary Taylor. Fillmore was a classic vice president—a relatively undistinguished man chosen to "balance the ticket" and help sway voters in his home state.

Fillmore's presidency was marked by the growing storm over the issue of slavery. He tried to straddle the controversy and succeeded in displeasing nearly everybody. He said, "God knows that I detest slavery, but it is an existing evil and we must endure it."

His own party refused to nominate him for the 1852 election. He left office under a cloud, literally as well as figuratively. His wife Abigail stood by his side during the cold downpour that marked his successor's inauguration. A few weeks later, she died of pneumonia. No wonder that the only reported ghost of Millard Fillmore is said to haunt the little house he built for his first wife. The Fillmore House in East Aurora, New York, is alleged to contain the spirits of both Millard and Abigail. They are not seen but heard. Their footsteps creak on the floors when no one is in that room. Low, indecipherable murmurings can be heard sometimes in the couple's bedroom. Theirs was a true love match.

Born in a log cabin to desperately poor parents, young Millard was sent to live with a wool carder as an apprentice, because his parents couldn't afford to feed all their seven children. A local judge saw Millard's potential and paid off his apprenticeship so he could at last go to school, where he fell in love with his teacher—Abigail. The couple delayed marriage until Fillmore had completed his law studies and established a profitable practice. They soon had a son and a daughter. The days in East Aurora were surely their happiest, which may explain their ghostly presence there.

So far, no one has reported Fillmore's ghost at his grave in Buffalo's Forest Lawn Cemetery. His tombstone, however, is the unusually frequent target of bird droppings, which might be an ironic tribute to the president's most famous diplomatic triumph. It seems that a dispute arose between Peruvian and American ship captains over the guano trade there. Guano is an incredibly rich and valuable fertilizer, an accumulation of centuries' worth of bird droppings in a waterless desert. Fillmore succeeded in negotiating the rights of Americans to participate in this lucrative trade. His enemies derided this as "Fillmore's Bird [Excrement] Treaty," but they didn't use the word "excrement." And so, to this day birds salute Fillmore's tombstone in an appropriate fashion.

Poor, unlucky Millard Fillmore seems to have created a dysfunctional family. Five years after the death of his first wife, he married a wealthy widow and built a mansion in Buffalo. At last free of money worries, Fillmore and his new wife became society leaders. After Fillmore died, however, his son, Millard Powers Fillmore, successfully sued his stepmother for control over his father's papers. The son then burned all these documents and letters, destroying any chance that historians could see Fillmore's side of his controversial administration and perhaps, more positively, reevaluate his presidency. Why would his only son want to consign his father's political career to the flames? Was Fillmore a fumbling failure as a father as well as a president? Or was he simply the unlucky victim of the curse of the number thirteen? Only the ghosts know for sure.

# Franklin Pierce

## 1804–1869
## 14th President, 1853–1857

---

Clad entirely in black, the mourning figure of a middle-aged woman sits at a desk, pen in hand. Heavy drapes cover the windows. A solitary candle casts a small pool of feeble light. "Dearest Benny," she begins to write, "Oh how I miss you, my beloved son." This infinitely sad scene of overwhelming grief was repeated every day in the White House from March 4, 1853, to March 4, 1857. Jane Appleton Pierce, wife of President Franklin Pierce, made a daily ritual of trying to communicate with her dead son. These solitary sessions were not really séances. True séances should have three or more participants, one of whom is a medium, a person especially sensitive to the spirit world, serving as the messenger between the living and the dead.

Jane Pierce's communion with her dead son was private and profoundly sad. She had borne three sons. Franklin Jr. lived only a few days; her congressman husband was in Washington at the time and never saw their firstborn son alive. A second son, Frank Robert, was born soon after her husband was elected the youngest man to serve in the Senate. The third son, Benjamin, known as "Benny," followed two years later. Jane persuaded her ambitious husband to retire from the Senate to live in New Hampshire with his growing family. Then four-year-old Frank died of typhus. Distraught, Jane persuaded Franklin to turn down President James K. Polk's offer to make him attorney general.

The Democratic Convention of 1852 was a notably contentious affair. The ultimate dark horse, Pierce was handsome, affable, and noncontroversial. He was chosen on the forty-ninth ballot. Jane fainted at the news. She prayed daily that her husband would lose the election, because she believed that their first two sons had been taken by God as punishment for her husband's ambitions. He won in a landslide.

Just weeks before his inauguration, Pierce, Jane, and eleven-year-old Benny were returning to New Hampshire from a holiday trip to Boston when their train derailed. In the wreck, Benny was killed, almost decapitated, before the eyes of his horrified parents, who were unhurt.

Jane never recovered from the shock. She believed that she was being haunted by the ghosts of her three dead sons, especially Benny. She became known as the "Shadow of the White House," refusing to appear in public. Secretary of War Jefferson Davis's second wife, Varina, took over some official hostess duties, good experience for her future role as First Lady of the Confederacy.

Did the ghosts of his sons haunt Pierce as well? A known alcoholic, Pierce started drinking heavily. Historians rank his presidency as a dismal failure. Both he and his wife were absolutely miserable in the White House. Asked what he would do after his own party refused to nominate him for reelection, Pierce said, "There is nothing left to do but to get drunk." Indeed, his was truly a haunted presidency.

# James Buchanan

## 1791–1868
## 15th President, 1857–1861

Was James Buchanan, fifteenth president of the United States, haunted by the spirit, or spirits, of deceased loved ones? Just why did the nation's only bachelor president never marry? There was a great deal of speculation and malicious gossip about Buchanan's love life, or lack of it, during his lifetime. His private life is still a mystery to historians.

What is certain about Buchanan's reputation is that most scholars rank him at the bottom of the list of presidents. Despite his impressive resume—House of Representatives from 1821 to 1831, U.S. Senate from 1834 to 1845, Secretary of State under James K. Polk, and Minister to the United Kingdom under Franklin Pierce—he proved a dismal failure as president. He was most unhappy during his one term. In his inaugural address, he repeatedly assured his audience that he would not run for reelection, a curious pledge from a new president. Four years later, he told President-Elect Abraham Lincoln, "If he [Lincoln] was as happy to be entering that office as he [Buchanan] was to be leaving it, he was indeed a most happy man."

Politically, Buchanan's White House years were haunted by the specter of disintegration of the Union; his appeasement of the South only delayed the coming storm. Personally, he was haunted by the deaths of his fiancée, Ann Caroline Coleman, and his close friend and longtime companion, William Rufus King. Most likely, Ann was a suicide. No one knows why William died so young.

Although Buchanan really was born in a log cabin, his parents were not poor, and he was able to graduate from Dickinson College. Family tradition claimed descent from King James I of

Scotland. Handsome, prosperous from his successful law practice, and always flirting with the ladies, Buchanan was a popular and highly intelligent man. He became engaged to Ann Coleman, whose father was a wealthy iron manufacturer. There were widespread rumors, however, that Buchanan was a shameless womanizer. When Ann learned that he visited a friend's wife when the husband wasn't home, Ann broke off the engagement. One week later, Ann was dead of an overdose of laudanum, opium dissolved in alcohol. Such dangerous drugs were not regulated at the time and were readily available over-the-counter. Ann's family forbade Buchanan's appearance at her funeral, despite his plea that both he and Ann were victims of malicious gossip. Buchanan swore that he would never marry because "all [my] love was buried in Ann's grave." He kept her letters with him for the rest of his life, directing that they be burned after his death.

Buchanan's other close relationship in life was with William Rufus King, with whom he shared a house when both men were senators. The two often attended events together; gossips called them "Buchanan and his wife." No one accused Buchanan of being effeminate, but Andrew Jackson, who never hesitated to express himself, called King "Miss Nancy" and "Aunt Fancy." King was elected vice president under Franklin Pierce, only to die shortly after taking office. All letters between he and Buchanan were burned after their deaths.

# Abraham Lincoln

## 1809–1865
## 16th President, 1861–1865

Abraham Lincoln believed that dreams could predict the future, if we knew how to interpret them. He always discussed his dreams with his wife, Mary, who shared his faith in dreams as messages from the future.

The night before his first inauguration, Lincoln dreamed that as he tied his black tie, preparing for his swearing in, he saw a double reflection in the mirror, both of his own face. The clearer image showed him absorbed in somber thought. The country that had elected him its leader was already showing signs of dividing; Lincoln knew that he faced a great challenge. Behind this first image was a second reflection, this one much fainter, pale and misty. This second image was of an exhausted, care-worn, grim version of himself. Mary's interpretation of his dream was that he would be elected to a second term, but that he would not live though it.

Lincoln's most widely reported dream came to him the night before his death. He dreamed that he was alone, walking in the central hall of the White House. In the distance he could hear faint sounds of weeping. "What happened?" he asked a passing servant. "The people are in mourning," was the reply. "Who is dead?" queried Lincoln. "The president." Then Lincoln saw his own body resting in an open coffin in the East Room. This tragic scene would soon become reality.

Lincoln's last cabinet meeting was held on the morning of his assassination. Cabinet members noted that the president, who usually focused intently on important questions, seemed distracted and moody. He described to them a dream, one which he said he'd had three nights in a row. In it, he was alone in a small boat on a dark and misty ocean. The boat had no oars and no rudder. Lincoln concluded the meeting by announcing, "Before long you will have important news." Then, he picked up his pen to sign the last document he would ever sign. According to the legend, it was an act creating the Secret Service, the agency that would later provide protection for the president.

As the Lincolns left the White House to go to Ford's Theater that evening, the guard at the front door said, "Good night Mr. President." Rather than his customary "Good night," Lincoln replied, "Goodbye," and proceeded to his rendezvous with death.

Lincoln was shot on the evening of April 14, a Good Friday. He drew his last breath early the next morning, never having regained consciousness. The cataclysmic event of Lincoln's assassination evoked an unprecedented outpouring of grief in the nation. The triumphant sense of relief that followed Robert E. Lee's surrender at Appomattox Courthouse was so suddenly eclipsed by the horror of assassination. The approaching end of the long national nightmare had produced only a brief respite of joy before the nation was plunged into a protracted spasm of mourning. The lost leader had been so foully shot down at his moment of vindication, his too brief moment of victory and relief at a successful conclusion of the titanic struggle to preserve the Union.

People everywhere wished an opportunity to honor the memory of their martyred president, and so began the longest ever farewell in American history. After lying in state in Washington for nearly a week, Lincoln's body was placed aboard his funeral train for the slow journey home. The route followed the heavily traveled northeast corridor from Washington to New York City, then up the Hudson Valley to Albany, then west to Springfield. At important cities along the way, the coffin was taken off the train and carried in solemn procession through the streets to some public building. The coffin was opened, and at each stop, thousands filed past to gaze on Lincoln's face. Again, the coffin would be returned to the train for the next leg of the twelve-day journey to Illinois.

Since 1865, thousands have been convinced that they've seen the phantom funeral train pass by. Many agree that their watches stopped for five to ten minutes as the ghost train steamed past. It is said that the ghost train simply levitates above any actual traffic on the line.

The ghost of the funeral train is said to roll down the tracks of its original route on an annual basis, between April 21, when the real train left Washington, and May 3, when it at last arrived at Lincoln's final resting place, his hometown of Springfield, Illinois. A spectral locomotive travels down the track first with only moderate speed, drawing no cars behind; it is the pilot engine, sent ahead of the actual funeral train to make certain that the right-of-way is clear. Most observers of the ghostly pilot locomotive and the train that follows it report a total and eerie silence enveloping their passage; others believe they've heard only a faint wail of an old-fashioned steam whistle.

Most sightings of the phantom train are at night or early in the morning. At night orange-red sparks fly out of the great flared smokestacks of the locomotives, and the reddish glow of open fireboxes can be seen reflected in the faces of the phantom engineer and fireman. The square headlights of the locomotives cast a pale yellow light on the line ahead.

On the funeral train, a lighted passenger car's windows reveal a massive coffin surrounded by an honor guard of soldiers, bareheaded, rifles at port arms. Some say that half the honor guard wear Union blue uniforms, the others, Confederate gray. A few observers claim that the honor guards are but skeletons, their naked skulls gleaming in the faint light.

Lincoln's ghost is the most famous of the many presidential ghosts. His spirit has been seen, or sensed, by many people over the years. Lincoln's ghost haunts the White House, as reported not only by staff and servants, but by several presidents, first ladies, and foreign dignitaries. Lincoln's ghost also has been reported at his home in Springfield, his tomb in Springfield, and at Ford's Theater, the place where he was shot by John Wilkes Booth.

Just why is Abraham Lincoln's ghost so famous? The widespread belief that his spirit still walks in the White House, the recurring appearances of the phantom funeral train, and the popular acceptance of his ghost appearance in Springfield and Ford's Theater all are related to his prominent place in American history and to his brutal assassination.

A very high proportion of ghosts are the results of sudden and violent deaths, especially murder. It appears as though the spirit is confused by being wrenched so abruptly from the living world that it wanders the earth, unable or unwilling to move on to the spirit realm. Sometimes this type of ghost is motivated by a thirst for revenge, but this does not coincide with Lincoln's persona or ghost. Another common motivation for ghosts is to help those left behind in the world of the living. These spirits try to carry on their lifetime missions to serve and protect. Typically, they appear to warn of impending danger or even suggest a solution to problems or threats. This type of apparition usually is called a "guardian spirit" and seems to fit well with Lincoln's alleged appearances in the White House, which seemed to reach a peak during the dark days of World War II.

Another reason behind the frequent appearances of Lincoln's ghost is the fact that the living man was interested in spiritualism. Mary Todd Lincoln was inconsolable after their son William ("Willie") died in the White House of typhoid. He was only eleven years old. Mary held at least eight séances in the White House's Green Room; her husband is known to have attended at least one. The president often visited the borrowed Washington crypt where Willie's body lay. He would request that the coffin be opened and would sit for hours trying to commune with his dead son.

Willie's ghost is said to have appeared to White House staff members during Ulysses S. Grant's presidency. More recently, Willie's ghost is supposed to have been heard moaning in the bedroom in which he died.

The first publicly acknowledged encounter with Lincoln's spirit in the White House occurred during Calvin Coolidge's presidency. His wife Grace saw Lincoln's figure in the Yellow Oval Room, which Lincoln had used as a library. The Great Emancipator was staring pensively out the window toward the southwest and Virginia. The phantom did not react to Grace's entrance, but just faded away.

Lincoln's ghost made several well-documented appearances in the White House during World War II. During a visit, Queen Wilhelmina of the Netherlands stayed overnight in the Rose Room, now the Queen's Bedroom. She reported that during the night, she heard a rap on the door. When she opened it, she was face to face with Lincoln, top hat and all. She immediately fainted. When she told her host and hostess, Franklin and Eleanor Roosevelt, of the experience, they were sympathetic, but not really surprised. Theodore Roosevelt had seen Lincoln's ghost in the White House but had not gone public with the story. He had, however, confided his experience to his cousin Franklin. Eleanor used the Lincoln Bedroom as a study and acknowledged sensing a presence looking over her shoulder as she read.

British prime minister Winston Churchill, on a wartime visit to the White House, had an interesting encounter with Lincoln's ghost. Late at night, Churchill had been enjoying a long soak in a hot bath, sipping a glass of scotch and smoking a cigar. Emerging from his bath, Churchill was surprised to see Lincoln standing by the bed. "I'm afraid you have me at a disadvantage, Mr. President," said the nude prime minister. Lincoln's phantom smiled slightly and evaporated.

Harry S. Truman recorded that he thought that Lincoln's ghost roamed the White House late at night. Once, Truman answered a late-night knock on his door only to find no one there. Then, his teenaged daughter Margaret had a White House sleepover with two friends; the girls got very little sleep because they heard footsteps when there was no one there. Truman was convinced it was Old Abe again. "The White House is haunted, sure as shootin'," Truman said.

Truman credits Lincoln's ghost with alerting him to the serious deterioration of the White House itself. What was Lincoln's ghost trying to tell him, he wondered, by the late-night footsteps and knocks on bedroom doors? Margaret Truman observed that the creaky floors made sounds of their own, especially when strong winds or thunderstorms occurred. Truman ordered an engineering survey of the then-149-year-old structure. The report was alarming: the wooden support posts and beams were deteriorated. "What is holding it up?" asked the president. "Mostly habit," was the reply. Truman ordered a complete reconstruction and credited Lincoln's spirit with delivering the message that the venerable house was in danger of collapse.

It is said that John F. Kennedy believed in life after death and attempted, privately, to communicate with Lincoln's spirit during meditation. It is not known if Lincoln's spirit responded in any way.

Ford's Theater, where the fatal bullet was fired into Lincoln's brain, is supposed to be haunted by the ghosts of both Lincoln and his assassin, John Wilkes Booth. In one version of the story, Booth is on stage, looking up to Lincoln in the presidential box. The two phantoms seem absorbed in debate. Others claim to have glimpsed the almost transparent forms of Lincoln and Booth engaged in conversation in the president's box.

During the tense years of the Civil War, Lincoln often said that he was looking forward to returning to his house in Springfield. There, he felt, he could truly relax and enjoy his family. By some accounts, Lincoln's ghost has done just that. His shade is said to appear in a rocking chair in his home, his face serene, his troubles past.

Lincoln's ghost has been seen, infrequently and only for the briefest of moments, in of all places the Confederate White House in Richmond, Virginia.

That Lincoln's spirit would materialize in the Confederacy's executive mansion might seem highly unlikely, but his real-life visit there in the closing days of the Civil War is a matter of historical record. The White House of the Confederacy still stands at Twelfth and Clay streets in Richmond. The three-story house, covered in gray stucco, was built in 1818 and became President

Jefferson Davis's official residence in August 1861 after the Confederate capital was moved from Montgomery, Alabama, to Richmond.

Davis had his office on the second floor; the first floor was devoted to official receptions and entertaining. In his office was an upholstered rocking chair that he favored for its comfort. When the Confederate government was forced to evacuate the capital, Davis had to flee on short notice, leaving behind his personal possessions, including his rocker. Lincoln visited Richmond on April 4, 1865, ten days before being gunned down in Ford's Theater. Characteristically, Lincoln came not as a triumphant conqueror but as a weary, much relieved leader, eager to confer with his generals on the problems of restoring peace and prosperity in the South. Lincoln brought along his young son, Tad, to tour the former Confederate seat of power. Lincoln is reported to have relaxed in Davis's rocking chair, pronouncing it "mighty comfortable."

The rocker is still there. So too, some allege, is Lincoln's spirit, quite literally in Davis's place, enjoying for a brief time the peace so hardly won.

Lincoln's phantom also has been spotted at his tomb in Springfield. Interestingly, Mary's ghost apparently has made few visits to the world of the living. She was intensely interested in spiritualism. She consulted spiritualists frequently, both before and after the assassination.

There is speculation that Mary was literally driven insane by grief. She survived her beloved husband by seventeen years, during which she made many attempts to communicate with the dead president, in addition to the three sons who predeceased her. Mary now rests contentedly in her tomb, surrounded by her husband and three of their sons, and she has no further need of mediums, spiritualists, or séances.

The ghost of Thomas "Tad" Lincoln, the youngest of the Lincolns' four sons, is a rare example of a playful, lighthearted spirit. Tad was the family clown and mischief-maker. He had a speech impediment, which may have helped earn him parental tolerance of his outrageous escapades. Tad's ghost is said to appear at the Equinox Resort in Vermont.

The Equinox Resort in Manchester is one of Vermont's oldest, most famous, and most prestigious hotels. In operation since 1769, it started as a country tavern where patriots plotted revolutionary actions over a few brews. The Equinox evolved into one of New England's most fashionable resorts in the nineteenth century, attracting the rich and famous to the picturesque little town of which it is the crown jewel.

Placed on the National Register of Historic Places in 1972, the Equinox has been resurrected as Vermont's most luxurious resort, providing its guests with the finest in accommodations, food, and entertainment . . . and ghosts. In keeping with its reputation, the ghosts of the Equinox include those of the highest social rank and claim to fame. None other than Mary and Tad Lincoln are among the many spirits encountered at the fabled majestic hotel.

It is said that on occasion the sounds of a sobbing child can be heard, accompanied by a mother's comforting voice, on the third floor. Some believe these ghosts to be those of Mary and Tad. Mary was a frequent guest at the Equinox. It was her refuge from the humid heat of Washington summers and the tensions of the wartime White House. Mary was so fond of the tranquil and luxurious Equinox, in fact, that she planned an extended vacation there with her husband in the summer of 1865 to help the president recover from the terrible strain of the Civil War. But that was not to be, as Lincoln died from the assassin's bullet early in the morning of April 15, 1865.

In the summer of 1862, Mary and Tad Lincoln arrived at the Equinox to gain a respite from mourning the death of Willie. Both Tad and Willie had been stricken with typhoid fever that previous winter, but Tad recovered and Willie died. Tad now had a classic case of survivor's guilt.

Willie and Tad had been known, affectionately, as the "tyrants of the White House" for their rambunctious sense of fun. They once organized a circus, featuring their menagerie of pets, on the White House roof, insisting that the entire staff as well as visitors attend performances. Tad once hitched his pet goat to a toy wagon and caused chaos at an official reception. The two irrepressible brothers had taken on themselves the job of lightening the somber pressures of the wartime White House.

Now only Tad was left. He threw himself into the role of family clown. Making his father laugh became his goal. At the Equinox, when Tad and his mother were joined by elder brother Robert, then a student at Harvard, Tad continued his playful pranks. A favorite was to sneak up behind a dignified adult, tap the person on the shoulder, and then race away.

Although Tad died in 1875 at the age of eighteen, visitors to the Equinox ever since have felt gentle taps on the back. But when they turn, they see no one. Is the ghost of Tad Lincoln still playing his tricks?

In contrast, the ghost of Robert, Lincoln's oldest son, is a study in dignified reserve. The distinguished-looking bearded gentleman, immaculately dressed in a business suit, waistcoat, and tie, paces the front terrace of an impressive Georgian Revival mansion, just south of Manchester, Vermont. Or rather, his ghost walks there, for Robert, the only son to live to maturity, died on July 25, 1926.

Robert's ghost wears a rather melancholy, reflective face, as he did in the few photographs for which he posed during his adult life. He had much to be sad about, despite having achieved great success as a business executive, diplomat, and high-ranking government official.

Why would the ghost of Lincoln's eldest son appear at this splendid house overlooking the Green Mountains? Robert loved the Vermont countryside more than any other place. He built Hildene, his twenty-three-room mansion, as a summer home, which also became his retirement home. He died at Hildene and was buried there briefly before his body was moved to Arlington National Cemetery as he requested in his will.

In addition to the tragedy of his father's brutal assassination, Robert had to cope with the deaths of his three younger brothers: Eddie at age three, Willie at age ten, and Tad at age eighteen. He was compelled, as well, to place his mother in a mental institution when she began wandering the streets, trying to sell her clothing under the unfounded delusion that she had no money. Also, Robert's only son, Abraham Lincoln II, died at age seventeen.

In personal accomplishments, Robert was an outstanding success. Following his graduation from Harvard, he joined General Ulysses S. Grant's personal staff and witnessed Lee's surrender at Appomattox. Invited to attend the theater with his parents on the evening of April 14, 1865, Robert declined and stayed in the White House because of exhaustion. He raced to his stricken father's bedside on hearing of the shooting and afterward lamented not being present to foil Booth.

In a spooky chain of events, Robert was present when both twentieth president James A. Garfield and twenty-fifth president William McKinley were shot. Robert was Garfield's secretary of war and was at arm's length when the president was shot in 1881 at a Washington train station. In 1901, McKinley had invited Robert to join him at the Pan-American Exposition in Buffalo. Robert didn't witness the shooting, but was nearby when the assassin fired a bullet into the president.

After serving as Benjamin Harrison's minister to Great Britain, Robert embarked on a career in business, becoming president of the Pullman Company, a leading corporation of the day. He also helped organize AT&T and the Chicago Commonwealth Edison. Republican Party leaders tried several times to get him to run for the White House, but Robert refused. He said that the politicians didn't want Robert Todd Lincoln to run, they wanted Abraham Lincoln's son to run. He believed that his father had much preferred Willie and Tad over him. His father even admitted that there was friction between them because, he said, "Robert is so much like me." Robert resented being able to see his father in the White House by appointment only, for ten minutes at a time, though the president would spend hours with his younger sons, even allowing Willie and Tad to interrupt cabinet meetings.

The three presidential assassinations traumatized Robert so that he began to fear being with the president in public. Was he some sort of magnet for assassins? He even chose to be buried in Arlington National Cemetery, his right as a former soldier, rather than join his parents and brothers in Springfield, Illinois.

In one final irony, the body of John F. Kennedy, the fourth victim of a presidential assassin, came to be buried about seventy yards from the grave of Robert Todd Lincoln. No wonder that Robert's spirit has chosen to haunt Hildene rather than the White House, Arlington, or Springfield.

An interesting footnote to Lincoln paranormal history is the ghost of Hannibal Hamlin, Lincoln's first vice president. It is alleged that his spirit haunts the house in which he died in Bangor, Maine. The ghost is that of a distinguished-looking Victorian gentleman, dressed in the severe black formalwear of the late nineteenth century. Although in life the man accomplished a great deal and was one of Maine's most famous native sons at the time, the ghost looks the picture of dejection, regrets, and depression. There is a good reason for this spirit to be so morose, for he very nearly was president of the United States.

President Hannibal Hamlin: the title sounded grand, but it never happened. Hamlin was born in 1809, the same year as Abraham Lincoln, in the tiny Maine town of Paris. Like Lincoln, his onetime hero and friend, Hannibal was a poor boy who worked his way out of poverty by educating himself in the law, becoming a successful lawyer before entering politics.

Folks in Maine did not hold with slavery. The few African Americans in the Pine Tree State were free men who worked hard and enjoyed the respect of their neighbors. Hamlin was elected to the Maine legislature as a Democrat who opposed slavery. When he went to Washington as a U.S. senator in 1848, he split with his fellow Democrats on the slavery issue, becoming a strong believer in the necessity of emancipation. Lincoln became a hero to Hamlin, and so he was deeply honored to be asked to run as Lincoln's vice-presidential candidate in 1860.

Hamlin was frustrated by the vice presidency, as indeed were most holders of that office. A loyal supporter of Lincoln, whom he considered a friend, Hamlin was most unpleasantly surprised when the Republican National Convention in 1864 dropped him from the ticket. Lincoln had said that he would leave the selection of a running mate up to the convention. The rumor was, however, that Lincoln believed that the ticket would be strengthened more by choosing Andrew Johnson as the running mate. A "War Democrat," Johnson had been the only southern senator to remain loyal to the Union. Lincoln believed that a national unity ticket with a southern Democrat would have the best chance of victory. And so Hamlin was dumped from the ticket. Embittered, he returned to the home in Bangor that he had purchased while vice president, and the Lincoln-Johnson ticket went on to victory, a victory that Hamlin helped secure by loyally campaigning for Lincoln.

Imagine Hamlin's tremendous sense of outraged disappointment when Johnson, vice president for only a month, was thrust into the presidency after Lincoln's assassination. If not for Lincoln's calculated decision to replace him on the ticket, Hannibal Hamlin of Maine would have been president of the United States.

And so Hamlin's ghost roams his Bangor home, head hanging low, sad eyes staring into infinity as he realizes just how close he came to the highest office in the land. His is a quiet, nonthreatening ghost who simply evaporates should he become aware of a living person near him.

# Andrew Johnson

## 1808–1875
## 17th President, 1865–1869

Abraham Lincoln was a tough act to follow for any man. The respect and admiration that the living president had earned had been transformed into a reverence for the slain leader's memory. It was Johnson's misfortune to enter the White House as a result of a truly cataclysmic event—the first-ever assassination of a president. Lincoln's true greatness and tragic death seemed to cast a shadow over Johnson's presidency. Johnson is best remembered as the first president to be impeached. Historians rank him among the worst presidents. Perhaps that explains why Johnson's home and grave have not been very popular with tourists.

Located in the heart of downtown Greenville, Tennessee, the home at the Andrew Johnson National Historic Site is not hard to find. While not handy to a major metropolitan center like George Washington's Mount Vernon, Greenville is in a popular and scenic tourist area, only about fifty miles from Dollywood and Great Smoky Mountains National Park.

Perhaps the site would attract more visitors if it were more widely known that the nation's seventeenth president may still be in residence—as a ghost. Johnson's apparition is not readily seen or sensed. There is nothing dramatic about it, just as there was nothing dramatic about the living man. This ghost reveals itself only to those who take the time to absorb the atmosphere of the house, those who can appreciate that Johnson most likely has been unfairly treated by both his contemporaries and history.

Johnson liked to sit in his upholstered lounge chair with its adjustable footrest. Some claim that his barely perceptible, almost transparent form can be seen in this almost modern-looking chair. Is that a glass in the spirit's hand or is that part of the vision influenced by Johnson's reputation as a drinking man?

His image as a drunk, like so many other aspects of his life, is based on misinterpreted or spurious facts. Often, Johnson is pictured as an uneducated bumpkin, totally unprepared for the office in which he was thrust. It is true that he had no formal education; his wife taught him to read and write. His long and active political career, however, took him from mayor of Greenville, the State House of Representatives, and the State Senate to governor of Tennessee and the U.S. Senate. He was no inexperienced newcomer to politics.

Born poor, Johnson was a staunch opponent of the South's plantation aristocracy. He was a populist whose background led him to become the only southern senator who remained loyal to the Union during the Civil War. Johnson was from the mountains of eastern Tennessee, where there were no cotton plantations and very few slaves. It was lowland western Tennessee that was part of the Cotton Kingdom. Johnson understood that slavery, in addition to being a moral evil, was bad economics for the poor whites whose interests he championed. Poor people, whether free blacks or whites, found it nearly impossible to compete with slave labor. Eastern Tennessee was antislavery, for the same reasons that Virginia's western mountains broke away from Confederate Virginia as the new Union state of West Virginia.

Ironically, Johnson got into political trouble by pushing Lincoln's stated agenda of a conciliatory policy toward the former Confederacy. The brutal assassination had turned the North's mood to revenge, while in contrast Johnson issued an unconditional amnesty proclamation on Christmas Day 1868. His real accomplishments include persuading France to withdraw its troops from their attempted empire in Mexico and his purchase of Alaska from Russia.

Johnson's image as a drunk was the result of an unfortunate incident at his inauguration as vice president. He was feeling miserable as a result of a bout of typhoid and drank some whiskey to dull the pain. He appeared unsteady on his feet and slurred his words. Lincoln defended Johnson against the resulting gossip, saying, "Andy is alright. I've known him for years. He likes a drink now and then but he's not a drunkard."

And so, if you take an opportunity to visit Johnson's home and sense his presence there, feel free to salute his memory with a glass of whiskey. Tennessee whiskey, if you please.

# Ulysses S. Grant

## 1822–1885
## 18th President, 1869–1877

The phantom is that of a distinguished looking, handsomely bearded man. He is seated comfortably in the type of wooden lounge chair known as an Adirondack, quite appropriate, as this is the Adirondack Mountains of northern New York state. The ghost's face wears an expression of satisfaction combined with complete exhaustion, but there is a hint of triumph there, too. The old warrior has just won his last battle, a battle to delay the Angel of Death.

The ghost should look a little familiar, at least if you are lucky enough to have a fifty dollar bill in your wallet. If the face matches, you may have just glimpsed the spirit of Ulysses S. Grant, Civil War hero, eighteenth president, and rather unexpectedly, successful author.

It should come as no surprise that the spirit of Grant should choose to appear here on the expansive porch of what is now known as the Grant Cottage State Historic Site atop Mount McGregor in the Adirondack Mountains near Wilton, New York. It was here, in the summer of 1885, that Grant finished writing his memoirs and then died. Grant had three great character traits—valor, determination, and perseverance. These had stood him well in his military career and were evident in his final battle, one against an implacable foe—throat cancer. His last months were a race against certain death; he was determined to finish his memoirs.

Grant's motivation to complete his book was love. He needed to ensure some income to his beloved wife, Julia. Julia had been a loyal and supportive wife through good times and bad. He could not bear the thought of her living in poverty after his death.

Like many great men, Grant had "married up." Born to humble parents, he wed the daughter of a wealthy St. Louis family. Julia had stayed at his side during the hard years. After resigning from the Army out of frustration with living in remote posts in the West with few advancement opportunities, Grant had pursued a variety of unsatisfactory jobs before rejoining the Army and rising to General in Chief.

Julia gloried in the good life. Unlike the many first ladies who regarded that position as a chore, she called her White House years a "wonderful dream" and thoroughly enjoyed her hostess duties. Upon leaving the White House, the Grants embarked on a two-year tour around the world; they were entertained lavishly everywhere. Their sudden descent into poverty was a result of Grant's involvement in a financial scandal. His son, Ulysses Jr., had persuaded his father to join his Wall Street brokerage firm and invest his life savings in it. Other partners turned out to be frauds and thieves, and the former president lost both his money and his reputation.

Then Grant was diagnosed with throat cancer. His many years of heavy cigar smoking—a wartime aide counted twenty cigars per day—had caught up with him.

Author Mark Twain, an admirer of the former president, offered to publish Grant's memoirs. The contract generously stipulated an unheard-of seventy-five percent royalty, but could the very sick man finish his book in a grim race against death?

A wealthy friend, Joseph Drexel, offered Grant the use of his mountaintop retreat. Grant moved in with his nurses and secretaries and wrote like he waged war—full speed, head on, and ultimately victorious. Grant finished his proofreading of the manuscript two days before he died. No wonder the Grant Cottage manifestation is exhausted but triumphant.

His book, published posthumously, was a great success. A bestseller, it sold 300,000 copies and earned his widow $450,000, a huge sum in those days. Not only was it popular, it was a huge success with the critics, who called it unsurpassed as military history, equal to Julius Caesar's accounts of his campaigns in Gaul.

The book restored Grant's reputation, which had been stained by the notorious corruption of his presidential administration, a result of Grant's misplaced trust in others. As was later the case with his Wall Street experience, Grant, who never would have dreamed of cheating, was not sufficiently cautious about trusting others.

To this day, at least many claim, his ghost relaxes on the porch of the cottage, serenely enjoying the view while aware of Death hovering nearby. His finest display of courage was in this last battle to ensure his wife's financial future. Some observers have noted the "thousand-yard stare" on Grant's face, as though his eyes are focused not on anything in this world, but on the spirit world to come.

The ghost of Grant also is alleged to haunt his mausoleum on Manhattan's west side. Grant's tomb is the largest mausoleum in America—a fitting tribute to the general who quite literally saved the Union. This version of Grant's spirit takes the form of the military leader at the height of his powers. This is the persona of the confident warrior who accepted Robert E. Lee's surrender at Appomattox Courthouse. This apparition is wearing a travel-stained, rather rumpled uniform, its boots are muddy, and cigar ash is dusted over his coat. His expression is one of calm courtesy, with no hint of arrogance. Grant had been ferociously belligerent in war. "This man fights. I cannot spare him,"

Lincoln replied to critics demanding he replace Grant on the grounds that his tactics were causing too many casualties. In victory, Grant was magnanimous. The surrender document that he wrote specifically prohibited any future prosecution of Confederate military personnel for treason, a clause which made it much easier for Confederates to honor the peace.

Although Grant was remarkably careless about his personal appearance—his wife Julia was always checking that all his buttons were buttoned—his outstanding leadership qualities were well organized. He has been underestimated as a visionary statesman. In his second inaugural address, for example, he stressed the need to protect the civil rights of former slaves and advocated federal legislation to ensure civil rights for all Americans.

If you should happen to spot Grant's ghost at Grant's cottage, Grant's tomb, or at the house in Galena, Illinois, given him by grateful citizens, you might salute him. In at least some respects, he was an underappreciated and farsighted leader as well as a heroic warrior. His shortcomings were overshadowed by memories of his greatness. His funeral was the occasion of a great outpouring of respect and admiration. President Grover Cleveland led 60,000 marchers in a funeral procession witnessed by two million Americans. It must bring a smile to the face of Grant's ghost that his final internment in his magnificent tomb was such a grand affair. It was a vindication of his reputation.

# Rutherford B. Hayes

## 1822–1893
## 19th President, 1877–1881

---

Officially, there is no ghost. "Ghost? What ghost?" is the likely reply of any guides or staff at the Rutherford B. Hayes Presidential Center in Fremont, Ohio. The home of the nation's nineteenth president is carefully preserved as a museum and memorial to a man whose reputation may have been unfairly maligned by the circumstances of his election.

Hayes's ghost, if indeed that is what or who it is, is not seen but rather sensed. Actually, this type of spirit is not uncommon in ghost legends. Many such stories feature an unseen spirit that makes itself known by very subtle changes in the spiritual atmosphere of a place. Some witnesses liken it to an air current that mysteriously moves by, seeming to brush along one's arm or fleetingly touch one's back. Someone, or something, is present but cannot be clearly identified by sight, hearing, smell, or touch. It's just there on the outer edge of our consciousness, an uneasy, slightly eerie experience.

Hayes's presence seems to center around the large oil portrait of the president on display in his house. Hayes called his estate Spiegel Grove. "Spiegel" is German for "mirror"; the water standing on the poorly drained land after a heavy rain reflected the sky like a huge mirror.

The mirror of history has not accurately reflected the true character and accomplishments of Hayes. He was one of the most honest men ever to reach the highest office in the land; his personal integrity is beyond doubt. And yet, he was called "Rutherfraud" by his enemies, or "His Fraudulency."

The election of 1876, the year of the nation's centennial, was unusually close. Democrat Samuel Tilden won the popular vote.

The Electoral College votes of four states— three of them southern states—were disputed. Voting irregularities were rampant.
Widespread fraud was charged. A congressional commission
was set up to decide the election.

Hayes would have seemed an unlikely recipient of southern
Democrat votes. A brigadier general for the Union in the Civil
War, Hayes had been wounded in action four times. A graduate
of Harvard Law School, he had been a congressman and governor of Ohio with a spotless reputation for honesty. He made few
enemies by being always open and friendly.

The congressional commission chose Hayes, undoubtedly
the result of a deal with southern Democrats. Hayes promised to
finally withdraw federal troops from the South, ending the
Reconstruction Era.

This backroom deal caused so much outrage that outgoing
president Ulysses S. Grant ordered a secret swearing-in of
Hayes in the Red Room of the White House on Sunday, March
4. He was fearful that mobs might disrupt the official inauguration on March 5. Insurrection was in the air, but Hayes's official
inauguration was held without serious incident.

Although Hayes's honesty in government was unquestioned,
he lived under a cloud of suspicion and resentment because of
his highly suspect selection by that corrupt congressional commission. It is certain that Hayes came to regret the unsavory
deal that put him in the White House. Does his ghost still brood
about his tarnished reputation? Many see deep sadness in his
haunted portrait at Spiegel Grove.

# James A. Garfield

## 1831–1881
## 20th President, 1881

James A. Garfield was a brilliant, multitalented man who pursued several careers before entering politics. Money was short in the Garfield household; his father died when James was seventeen months old. Garfield worked his way through Hiram College as a janitor, transferring to Williams College for graduation as a Minister of the Gospel, the only licensed preacher to make it to the White House. He may have had the highest IQ of any president. His favorite party trick was to be asked a question in English. He then would write out the answer simultaneously using both hands, one writing in Latin and the other in ancient Greek.

A major general in the Civil War, Garfield was elected a state senator and a U.S. congressman before emerging as a dark horse candidate for president. Foreshadowing the John F. Kennedy assassination eighty-two years later, Garfield was a very popular, handsome young president when he was shot down on July 2, 1881.

Is it possible for one ghost to haunt several different locations? If it is, do the spirits travel instantaneously? Many believe that ghosts choose to appear, if at all, at places that had special meaning to the living person or where the body is buried.

The phantom of Garfield has been seen at various times in the White House and in Ohio in his last home in Mentor and at Hiram College. His ghost, some claim, has also been seen at Elberon on the New Jersey shore, where he died.

This Elberon ghost was seen most frequently in the closing decades of the nineteenth century, although a few sightings have been reported in recent years. Perhaps this spirit is no longer as restless as he once was, for his tragic death took place more than 125 years ago.

A tall, distinguished-looking gentleman strolls slowly along Ocean Avenue near the intersection with Lincoln Avenue. His receding hairline gives him the appearance of having a high, domed forehead. He has a mustache and full beard, in the high fashion of the Victorian Era. His seaside walks appear to take place mostly in late evening during summer and early fall. The apparition seems to take no notice of anyone else, but if approached, it dissolves in the salt air. Those who have seen the ghost believe it is that of Garfield, who died there on September 19, 1881.

Why would President Garfield's ghost still wander along the seashore at Elberon? This was his favorite resort, and it was the place of his death following a long, painful struggle with the wounds he received from an assassin's bullet. Only a few months after his inauguration, Garfield was shot with a .44-caliber pistol while in Washington's train station. It was an abdominal wound, one that did not kill him right away.

All deaths by violence are tragic, but Garfield's agonizing death was especially sad because better medical care could have saved his life. It is a curiosity that out of four U.S. presidents who have been assassinated, two were from Ohio, Garfield and William McKinley. These presidents shared other common circumstances. Both were wounded by the assassin's bullet and both survived for a time, though critically wounded—McKinley for a few days and Garfield for more than two months. Whereas Lincoln and Kennedy both suffered massive head wounds that they could not have survived, McKinley and Garfield probably could have been saved if modern antibiotics were available.

Although many Civil War veterans at the time were walking around with bullets lodged in them, Garfield's doctors probed endlessly with nonsterile fingers and instruments, trying to retrieve the bullet. In doing so, they spread the infection, which eventually overwhelmed the president. At his trial, the assassin, Charles Guiteau, commented that it was Garfield's doctor, not the bullet, which really killed him. True, but it was beside the point. Guiteau was executed. As it was, the president lingered, in great pain but lucid, for seventy-eight days after being shot.

Most of those days were spent near Long Branch, in a cottage on the grounds of the old Elberon Hotel, long since demolished. The White House had been judged inappropriate for Garfield's feverish convalescence, as Washington was notoriously hot and humid, a miserable climate in the days before air-conditioning. Garfield had enjoyed the cool ocean breezes at Long Branch on vacation, so why not try to recover at the Jersey shore? The ailing president finally died from massive infection, as he gazed out the window of his seafront cottage by the ocean he had always loved to visit.

In their fascinating book, *Haunted America*, authors Michael Norman and Beth Scott recount the experiences of some recent occupants of a cottage once occupied by James and Lucretia Garfield when James taught at Hiram College from 1856 to 1866. In the cottage, lights turn on and off by themselves. Water runs from faucets without being turned on. Some rooms become unaccountably frigid in the middle of summer. Although no one in the house smokes, strong cigar odors are common—and Garfield smoked cigars.

A number of recent sightings suggest that at least on occasion, Garfield's ghost chooses to haunt his tomb in Cleveland's Lakeview Cemetery. Some think that his spirit began to haunt the tomb after his beloved wife joined her martyred husband in death, having outlived him by thirty-six years. Now, almost 130 years after his agonizingly prolonged struggle with infection, Garfield's ghost is said to roam about his impressive memorial, a tower 50 feet in diameter and 180 feet high, with a chapel that holds his casket.

# Chester A. Arthur

## 1829–1886
## 21st President, 1881–1885

It is late at night in Washington and quiet on the edge of Lafayette Square. Across the square, the White House gleams, its walls brilliantly lit by floodlights. Here, the relative gloom is broken by a beautiful stained glass window, lit from within the church that stands at 16th and H streets.

The figure of a man slowly strolls up toward the church, coming from the direction of the White House. His attention obviously is focused on the stained glass window. Tears seem to glisten in each eye as he stares intently at the window. At six feet, two inches tall, the same height as George Washington, he makes an impressive figure. What really stands out, however, is his facial hair; he wears a mustache, but while his chin is clean-shaven, his handsome face is framed by bushy muttonchops. He is elegant in an immaculate suit of high Victorian fashion.

As though becoming aware of another person in his vicinity, he turns and locks eyes briefly and then suddenly vanishes. The living bystanders have just encountered the ghost of President Chester A. Arthur, the man who commissioned the memorial stained glass window.

Arthur was the fourth man, out of a total of eight, to be thrust into office by the death of his predecessor. Folks had low expectations of the new president. He was regarded as a hack politician, the product of a notoriously corrupt New York political machine. He appeared to be the poster child for unabashed patronage and unsavory backroom deals. Ulysses S. Grant had appointed Arthur customs collector for the Port of New York, a plum job with many opportunities for political payoffs. Rutherford B. Hayes had fired Arthur from that job, favoring a merit-based, nonpolitical civil service.

More than one politician is said to have exclaimed in horror, "Oh my God, Chet Arthur is president!" on learning of Garfield's death. But, Arthur's presidency turned out to be a big surprise—a pleasant surprise. He became a crusader for civil service reform and ran an efficient, scandal-free administration.

A few witnesses claim to have encountered Arthur's ghost at his birthplace in the remote rural area near Bordoville, Vermont. He is an unmistakable ghost, because he is always dressed immaculately. Known as "Elegant Arthur," he reportedly owned seventy pairs of trousers. He hated looking rumpled, so he changed clothes several times a day. That might sound like he was a superficial dandy, but he, in fact, possessed a substantive sense of justice. As a young lawyer, he volunteered to represent an African-American woman who was refused a seat on a streetcar because of her race. He won the case for her.

Arthur's three-and-a-half years in the White House were lonely for him. His beloved wife, Ellen Herndon Arthur, died suddenly at the age of forty-two, twenty months before he succeeded Garfield. Overwhelmed by grief, Arthur refused to even consider dating another woman. He commissioned, as a memorial to his wife, the lovely stained glass window at the "church of the presidents," St. John's Episcopal Church. St. John's has been visited at least once by every president from James Madison to Barack Obama. Built in 1815, it was designed by Benjamin Latrobe, the architect of the U.S. Capitol.

When the memorial window had been installed, Arthur requested that the church be lit all night so that he could see "Ellen's window" from his White House office across the square. A night owl, Arthur would work until the early morning hours and then sleep until noon. He liked to go on late-night walks, frequently across the square to St. John's to admire the memorial window up close. This made him feel, he said, closer to Ellen. Evidently, his spirit still makes that lonely nightly vigil at St. John's.

# Grover Cleveland

## 1837–1908
## 22nd President, 1885–1889,
## and 24th President, 1893–1897

Most museums can seem a little spooky at night. The reduced lighting seems to cast wavering shadows. That skeleton of a Tyrannosaurus rex could not possibly have moved, could it? Is it just imagination or did that stuffed tiger just lick its chops? The display of Egyptian mummies causes an involuntary collage of scenes from countless horror movies to cross one's consciousness.

These spooky feelings reach a crescendo in a museum that, in full daylight and in company of others, presents a truly macabre array of nightmarish specimens, models, and pictures of human anatomical oddities. As author Gretchen Worden observed, "In most museums you go to look at objects. In the Mutter Museum sometimes the objects seem to be looking at you."

The intended audience for Dr. Thomas Mutter's collections of unique pathological specimens was physicians and medical students. If, however, museums can be said to have cult followings, the Mutter Museum at the College of Physicians of Philadelphia would qualify. Ghoulish curiosity would score high as a motive for nonphysicians to tour the exhibits of deformed and diseased bodies and body parts. Do the spirits of the dead whose pathetic or fatal abnormalities have become museum exhibits ever roam these halls? Many suspect so. Among these spirits is alleged to be the phantom of President Grover Cleveland.

Cleveland's ghost might prowl the Mutter Museum to visit the piece of his upper jaw that resides there. Surgeons and medical examiners apparently liked to keep little souvenirs from famous patients or corpses. Hence, along with a chunk of Cleveland, the Mutter Museum displays John Wilkes Booth's thorax, Chief Justice John Marshall's bladder stones, and supposedly, Wolfgang Amadeus Mozart's skull.

Among ghost stories, there is a recurrent theme of specters showing interest in reuniting with, or at least viewing, missing limbs or body parts. Cleveland's partial upper jaw had to be removed surgically in 1893 because of a cancerous tumor. This surgery was performed in secret aboard a yacht cruising Long Island Sound. The country was in the midst of a severe financial crisis. Cleveland was concerned that the news he was undergoing cancer surgery would increase public panic, so the cover story was that he was on a vacation cruise. Not even Cleveland's vice president knew about the procedure. The full story wasn't told until nine years after Cleveland's death.

It is claimed that Cleveland's phantom drops by now and then to stare curiously at his carefully preserved tumor. The figure is that of a tall, distinguished-looking man. His build would be described diplomatically by clothing salesmen as "portly"; the rest of us would say "really fat." He had a "beer belly," which he acquired the traditional way—by drinking beer. He and his law partner, Oscar Folsom, once promised one another to limit daily beer consumption to three glasses, but they got really thirsty. What to do? They went out and bought twenty-eight-ounce glass beer mugs.

Cleveland is remembered mostly as the only president to serve two nonconsecutive terms and the only president to actually get married in the White House. In the Blue Room ceremony, the forty-nine-year-old president wed the twenty-one-year-old daughter of his best friend. Frances Folsom had been unable to attend Cleveland's first inauguration because her college wouldn't excuse her from class that day. Frances gave birth to her second daughter in the White House. Some claim to have heard her ghostly childbirth cries coming from a second-floor bedroom.

Cleveland's portly spirit is said to haunt his birthplace, the former Presbyterian Manse at 207 Bloomfield Avenue in Caldwell, New Jersey. Now a national historic site, the house is open to tours. Ghost sightings are not guaranteed and are, in fact, rarely reported.

# Benjamin Harrison

## 1833–1901
## 23rd President, 1889–1893

Benjamin Harrison believed in ghosts. It has been documented that he believed he was visited by his father's ghost. He also encountered the specter of his wife Caroline, who died in the White House of tuberculosis on October 25, 1892, just days before he lost his bid for reelection. Harrison's chances at a second term really died along with Caroline. Distraught by his beloved wife's long battle with her disease, he did not actively campaign and was defeated by the man he had beaten four years earlier, Grover Cleveland.

While Caroline's ghost most likely was a pathetic, gentle spirit, the ghost of Harrison's father was more the stuff of nightmares. Just west of Cincinnati, in the town of Addyston, is an imposing monument to Benjamin's grandfather, William Henry Harrison, war hero and the first Ohioan to become president of the United States. Only two hundred feet to the west lies the grave of William's son and Benjamin's father, John Scott Harrison. This site reportedly is haunted by his truly gruesome ghost.

The ghost of John Scott Harrison doesn't appear as often as it once did, which may be just as well for the mental health of passersby. This ghost is as unique in his appearance as in his personal history. He is a slightly phosphorescent spirit seen sitting atop his tombstone, alert and aggressively staring at any who approach. He holds a large revolver in his right hand, but what makes this ghost really different is that only his head and limbs are intact. His chest is empty, the ribs torn open. His torso is missing, with only his spine visible where his abdomen should be, earning this spirit the nickname "Gutless Ghost." There is an interesting story behind this phantom's missing body parts and his brandishing a gun.

President William Henry Harrison, who died after only thirty days in office, fathered ten children, only one of whom, John, outlived him. John served two terms in Congress but spent most of his life as a successful farmer. His major claim to fame is that he is the only son of a president to have fathered a president.

John was buried practically in the shadow of his famous father's tomb in 1878, but he didn't stay there. His son Benjamin was tipped off that his father's body had been stolen by grave robbers and sold to the Cincinnati Medical School. The future president, furious at this indignity to his father, stormed into the school and discovered his father's partially disemboweled corpse hidden in a dumbwaiter. There was no way to identify his father's organs, now scattered among other medical specimens, so what was left of John was placed back in his coffin for reburial. That night, the story goes, his ghost appeared to his son suggesting that a loaded revolver be placed in the coffin as a symbol of his spirit's determination to stay in his grave. Benjamin accordingly put a Colt .38 in the coffin. So the Gutless Ghost remains at the grave, making infrequent but horrible appearances.

Benjamin Harrison, although haunted by ghosts in his lifetime, appears as a ghost himself only on rare occasions. There have been only a few, unsubstantiated apparitions at his home in Indianapolis, now open to the public. He died of flu and pneumonia in his house on March 13, 1901. Those who claim to have briefly glimpsed his spirit recall a wracking cough from his tormented, eerily glowing form.

# William McKinley

## 1843–1901
## 25th President, 1897–1901

It would have helped, of course, if the doctors could have seen what they were doing. Just where was that bullet, and how much damage had it done? Although electric lights were no longer a novelty, and the exhibit halls and auditoriums of the Pan-American Exposition were lavishly supplied with thousands of electric lights, the small room in which the doctors were examining their patient was lit only by gas jets, which could not be used. The anesthesia in use was ether, which is dangerously explosive near open flames. Desperate, the doctors resorted to using mirrors to reflect sunlight.

The date was September 6, 1901, the place was Buffalo, New York, and the unfortunate gunshot victim was President William McKinley. In an eerie foreshadowing of the John F. Kennedy assassination sixty-two years later, the first bullet was not the fatal one. Among the what-ifs of history is the question of whether faster reaction by his guards could have prevented the second shot or deflected its trajectory. (Following McKinley's death, the Secret Service was assigned full-time protection of the president, with a larger budget and better training.)

The fatal bullet was not located until the autopsy; it had penetrated the president's stomach, kidney, and pancreas. McKinley died of gangrene poisoning, an agonizing eight days after the shooting. There is no doubt that modern surgical techniques, together with antibiotics, could have saved him.

As he lay slowly dying, McKinley is said to have confided to his wife, Ida, and close friends that he was being visited by supernatural visitors he called "angels." The angels were the spirits of his two dead daughters. His second-born, also named Ida, had lived only five months. The first, Katie, had died of typhoid fever at the age of four. Other angels, his parents, also appeared at the dying president's bedside. Had these angels been reassuring about the afterlife? McKinley faced death with composure. His last words were, "This is God's will."

McKinley's own spirit is believed to appear as a translucent, shadowy form at his gravesite in Canton, Ohio. Another spirit, that of McKinley's wife, Ida, is said to appear there as well.

This pathetic ghost is seldom seen these days, though it once was a commonly reported apparition. Perhaps her spirit finally has found peace a century after her death. Ida's ghost is a non-threatening, gentle spirit that evokes only sympathy in the hearts of any who see it, especially those familiar with her story.

Ida Saxton was the sophisticated, well-educated daughter of a banker when she met William McKinley, a young ambitious lawyer and Civil War hero. The young couple's married life was clouded by tragedy, as both their daughters died early in their lives. It is said that the trauma of losing her second offspring at the age of five months brought about the first of a lifetime of epileptic seizures and fragile health for Ida. The stresses of the White House social life were particularly hard on her. She customarily clutched a small bouquet while seated in a chair in a receiving line so that she wouldn't have to shake hands, revealing her trembling limbs. When, as happened often at state dinners, she passed out briefly, eyes rolling back in her head, her husband would place a handkerchief over her stricken face and continue conversation. Guests would politely ignore the incident until her recovery. The president was always tenderly protective of her. When he was gunned down, McKinley's first words to an aide as he lay in a pool of blood were about his concern for his wife. "Be careful how you tell her," he whispered to his secretary. "She's not strong, you know."

Ida outlived her assassinated husband by six years and eventually was buried beside him and their infant daughters. Her ghost is said to sit by the graves of her husband and children, holding a bouquet and trembling visibly. If you see her grieving spirit, kindly avert your eyes from her handicap.

# Theodore Roosevelt

## 1858–1919
## 26th President, 1901–1909

Sagamore Hill, the house that Theodore Roosevelt built in 1885 and lived in until his death in 1919, offers many insights into his character and interests. Decorated in a strongly masculine style with many hunting trophies—bearskin and zebra rugs, mounted heads of lions, elephant tusks, and so on—the sprawling Queen Anne–style mansion practically reeks of testosterone. Like all successful politicians, "TR," as he liked to be called, consciously and deliberately created his public persona. In his case, it was an image of a vigorous, adventurous, and aggressive alpha male, the epitome of masculinity.

TR dealt with a hidden fear most of his life, a fear that he would not earn or deserve his father's approval. Early on, he determined to personify manliness as he understood it; his fear of showing weakness shaped his life, especially emotionally. His compulsion to have his sons personify manliness contributed to the tragedy that produced the ghost that haunted his last six months of life.

TR was the second child, but first son, born to a wealthy and influential New York family. As a small child, he suffered from severe asthma. Struggling for each breath is a searingly traumatic experience. Little Ted was puny, sickly, and timid. This last trait was particularly bothersome to his father, whom he practically worshipped. Somehow Teddy perceived that his father was concerned that his son might be deficient in manliness. The little boy was given a set of weights with which to "build himself up." A boxer was hired to provide lessons in self-defense. Teddy got the message—real men are strong, brave, and adventurous, and every dad wants his sons to be masculine role models. Ted set to work to live up to his father's ideal of a son.

Puny little Ted eventually became TR, the leader of men, the hunter of fierce wild animals, and the courageous, rather reckless military hero. The specter of his father's subconscious doubts about his so-called manliness was in the background throughout TR's life.

In 1884, at the age of twenty-five, TR experienced a kind of perfect storm of emotional trauma. His mother died on February 14 (his father had died when TR was in college). That same day, only a few hours later, his wife, Alice Lee Roosevelt, died of kidney disease complicated by childbirth, leaving a two-day-old daughter to raise. TR had a breakdown. He left his infant girl in the care of his sister and left town. He just could not handle his wife's untimely death; he never spoke her name again, and there is no mention of her in his autobiography. He buried his grief, unable or unwilling to show "weakness" by crying. His firstborn, Alice, thought he had abandoned her emotionally. She grew up to be a rather cold, unhappily married gossip of renown. A specially embroidered pillow on her sofa read, "If you can't say anything nice about anybody, come sit by me."

TR's second marriage to Edith Carow produced four sons and another daughter. Each son learned early in life that fearless adventurism was the way to win their father's approval. Roughhousing and participation in highly competitive and rather risky impromptu games was expected. The whole family would go on strenuous hikes, often inviting government officials and diplomats to tag along, if they had the stamina. The British ambassador is said to have told a friend, "You must understand that the president is about eight years old."

The athletic antics of the younger Roosevelts, combined with their devil-may-care disdain for restraining rules, could get out of hand. The four boys and a handful of friends became known as the "White House Gang." At one point the chief usher had to issue a ruling: playing pirates in the East Room was okay, but water guns were out. TR Jr. took such breathtaking chances that his parents began to wonder if he'd make it to adulthood. The sons of high-achieving fathers are always under pressure to measure up to dad; this was especially true in the Roosevelt family. As TR Jr. later wrote, "Don't you think that it handicaps a boy to be the son of a man like my father and especially to have the same name? Don't you know there can never be another Theodore Roosevelt?"

TR Jr. went on to become a much-decorated war hero in both World Wars, earning a posthumous Congressional Medal of Honor. The youngest son, Quentin, also displayed the bravery under fire expected of TR's sons. It got him killed at the age of twenty, and his tragic death came to haunt his father, quite literally.

Quentin, full of mischief and disdain for convention, was the family clown. Most of the time, he could charm everyone into overlooking his misadventures. Once, he seriously damaged a full-length portrait of onetime first lady Lucy Hayes by running into it with his wagon. Dad, normally tolerant of collateral damage from rigorous play, was furious about this injury to government property. "Too reckless," decreed TR. The president was worried that Quentin was cowardly in family pillow fights; he quickly retreated to a fetal position for defense. TR confided to his other sons that little Quentin "seemed a little soft." This devastating doubt about this manliness was quickly communicated to Quentin. Quentin decided to become the bravest of the brave.

He finally earned his father's unreserved praise when as a fighter pilot in World War I, he shot down an enemy plane. His father was exultant, proud that "the last of the lion's brood had been blooded." Quentin, whose commanding officer had warned him about taking too many chances, became more reckless, even foolhardy, in his tactics. He took on two German opponents at the same time. He was shot down and died. The official German report characterized him as "brave but inexperienced."

TR was devastated by the news of Quentin's death. Had he somehow, inadvertently, contributed to his death by demanding more and more evidence of "manliness?" Did Quentin, desperate for approval and reassurance about this masculinity, deliberately run outrageous risks?

It is said that, every night for the rest of his life, TR was haunted by a vision of his son in a bloody flying uniform. "Did I do well? Was I a brave boy?" asked the ghost. Wracked by doubts and regret, TR survived his youngest son by only six months. The official cause of death was a coronary embolism. Most would say it was a broken heart.

Some say that TR's ghost still sits in his second-floor study at Sagamore Hill. His spirit is brooding, remembering a long and active life, but one ending in family tragedy.

Roosevelt's tenure in office was marked by a new activism in limiting the power of large corporations, conserving the nation's natural resources, and asserting international leadership backed by an expanded and modernized navy. TR's sudden death aborted his planned run for the presidency again—a race he likely would have won.

# William Howard Taft

## 1857–1930
## 27th President, 1909–1913

It is nearly dusk at the gravesite overlooking Theodore Roosevelt's home, Sagamore Hill, near Oyster Bay, New York. A tall, rather stout figure appears as a faintly shimmering mist, difficult to see in the gathering gloom. The phantom appears to be downcast, obviously standing in mournful tribute to the grave's occupant, Roosevelt himself. The ghostly mourner is none other than William Howard Taft, TR's best friend. There were, however, a number of years when the two friends were bitter enemies rather than steadfast friends. Their final reconciliation came almost too late, only months before TR's death.

The tragic ghost standing lonely sentry duty at the grave might be motivated by profound regret—regret about what might have been. The two old friends had wasted about nine years in a feud based on political differences that literally changed history. The characters of these two men both featured strong egos and contrasting emotional personalities that contributed to their years of hostile distrust.

TR's image was that of a boisterously aggressive, dramatically self-confident leader. He liked to compare himself to a lion. When he died, the son who had been at his bedside telegraphed to his brothers, "The old lion is dead."

Taft, in contrast, was a quietly dispassionate, deliberative man, appropriate to being a judge, which he was for much of his life. Once, when Taft was asked if his presidential policies would differ from those of his predecessor and mentor, TR, he replied that he would try to follow the same goals, but "without all the noise."

Noise just wasn't in his makeup. He had been an Ohio Supreme Court judge and solicitor general of the United States, and he served on the U.S. Court of Appeals when President William McKinley appointed him governor-general of the Philippines. Roosevelt made Taft secretary of war and hand-picked him as his successor. Taft won the 1908 election; it was only the second time he had run for office.

When Roosevelt discovered that Taft had strong opinions of his own and was not a Roosevelt clone, he ran against Taft as a third-party candidate in 1912. Splitting the Republican vote resulted in the victory of Democrat Woodrow Wilson, a win which greatly surprised and disappointed both Taft and Roosevelt. They didn't speak for years. Then, when Roosevelt's youngest son, Quentin, was killed in action, Taft wrote his former friend a heartfelt letter of condolence. This sparked a renewal of their friendship. The reconciliation was eerily similar to the relationship of John Adams and Thomas Jefferson. Those two, former close friends during the American Revolution, had become bitter rivals when Jefferson defeated Adams in the election of 1800. Their friendship resumed after Jefferson wrote to console Adams on the untimely death of his daughter, Abigail Adams Smith.

When Roosevelt died less than six months after the two old friends reconciled, Taft was distraught. At Roosevelt's funeral, Taft stayed by the grave long after the other mourners had left. Perhaps, in spirit, he never left his friend alone again.

# Woodrow Wilson

## 1856–1924
## 28th President, 1913–1921

There is another presidential home in Washington other than the White House. It now is a national historic site. It is Woodrow Wilson's retirement home at 2340 South Street N.W., and like the White House, some believe it to be haunted.

Almost transparent, the pale gray figure is seated at the former president's desk. He appears to be wearing a dress shirt, tie, and jacket. The lower part of his body is covered in an old-fashioned lap robe or blanket. The phantom's face is disfigured by the sagging muscles on the left side, symptoms of a paralytic stroke. The unaffected side of the ghostly visage is marked by a frowning, far-off stare, as though the onetime president were remembering his one great failure as chief executive. This ghost has appeared to only a few recently. Perhaps the spirit of Wilson has found peace at last.

Peace, a truly lasting peace among nations, was Wilson's goal in the last years of his presidency. Before he left the White House, however, he knew in his heart that he had failed in his quest to prevent the kind of cataclysmic war that had just ended from ever breaking out again. Years before his death, Wilson became a man haunted by the specters of failure and of future wars.

Many historians assert that World War II was a rematch of World War I. Germany's loss in the first was followed by a vindictive peace treaty that contributed to its determination to overturn what most Germans came to regard as an unfair resolution.

In Paris, Wilson was unable to persuade his victorious allies to conclude a peace treaty unencumbered by vengeance. This first critical failure may have been the result of a stroke, one that was undiagnosed or carefully covered up by his doctors and advisers. Officially, the president was stricken by flu. Many associates noted, however, a distinct change in personality after his illness. He became suspicious, secretive, and egocentric. His speech became flat, without inflection or emotion. These characteristics are all symptoms of a stroke affecting the brain.

On his return home, Wilson embarked on a strenuous and ultimately unsuccessful campaign to sway public opinion to support his dream project—a league of nations to avoid future wars. He then had a severe stroke in September 1919, nineteen months before the end of his term. Effectively, his wife ran the government while Wilson was incapacitated by his second stroke. The first apparent stroke in Paris may have produced brain damage that should have led to his vice president taking over. But, before the 1967 ratification of the Twenty-Fifth Amendment to the Constitution, the succession in case of a president's incapacity for any reason was not clearly stated. What neurologist would be brave enough to state that the president had suffered serious brain damage?

Wilson was in denial about his stroke and even wanted to run for a third term. He was a bitter, broken man in retirement, caged in his own crippled body and haunted by his own failures. A lifelong student of history and politics, Wilson could foresee, but do nothing to prevent, another world war. No wonder his ghost is so despondent.

# Warren G. Harding

## 1865–1923
## 29th President, 1921–1923

In common with James Madison, Warren G. Harding's ghost is outshined by that of his wife. Dolley Madison's phantom is one of Washington's most famous and frequently seen ghosts. The specter of Florence Kling Harding appears in the hotel in which her husband died and at the home they shared in Marion, Ohio.

San Francisco's Palace Hotel is a well-known landmark just east of Union Square and New Montgomery Street. This grand hotel has an interesting history. The original structure was destroyed by fire in the 1906 earthquake. According to legend, the present building was completed in 1909 using the salvaged steel frame of the original. The beautifully restored Palace offers all the amenities a contemporary guest could wish for, and its more than five hundred units are renowned for their peaceful luxury. Not only is the sound insulation quite effective, but staff and guests alike have been admonished to be quiet by a very determined ghost.

The experience of a recent guest is typical. She was walking down the corridor on the eighth floor with her admittedly rambunctious little boy in tow. Suddenly, a very stern-looking woman in her sixties appeared. She was wearing a dress draped in beads of the style popular in the 1920s. Her hair was styled in tight waves. Steel-rimmed glasses framed her fiercely glaring eyes. A thrusting jaw and beaklike nose completed her aggressive persona.

"Quiet!" she demanded. "The president is resting!"

"The president of what?" asked the impudent youngster.

"The president of the United States!" was the rejoinder. Duly impressed, mother and child tiptoed quietly to the elevator.

When the guest asked a bellboy when the president had arrived at the Palace, she was met with a blank stare.

"What president?" he asked. "We don't have a president here now." The guest later was informed by a friendly chambermaid that her encounter was not all that unusual.

"Oh, that's just Mrs. Harding's ghost. We see her whenever there's noise in the halls."

Known as "the Duchess," Florence Harding, like her ghost, was strong-willed and outspoken. In the contemporary age of intense and intrusive press scrutiny of political candidates and their families, Florence's lurid past, if revealed, could have kept her husband out of the White House. She had an illegitimate child with another man before she wed Harding. Her son's father never married her, and the son died at age thirty-five from alcoholism and tuberculosis, alone and in poverty, far from the glamour of the White House.

Florence was a very assertive first lady who was fiercely protective of her husband, as well as aggressively ambitious for him. She said, "I have only one real hobby—my husband!" She is quoted as telling him, "Well, Warren, I have got you the presidency; what are you going to do with it?"

Harding died suddenly, and some say mysteriously, at the Palace Hotel on August 2, 1923. The exact cause of death is not known, as Florence forbade an autopsy, and no one, including new president Calvin Coolidge, had the nerve to override her decision. At the time, there were suspicions that Florence had poisoned her husband. Her supposed motive was to spare him the disgrace and possible impeachment that could have followed when the many scandals of his corrupt and inept administration came to light.

Visitors to the Harding Home in Marion who make negative comments about America's twenty-ninth president may feel a painful rap on the elbow or knee. Unkind words about Harding can mysteriously lead to a stumble on the porch steps or a flat tire in the parking lot. One tourist even claimed that his new car was deliberately scratched in the parking area behind the house after he made crude jokes about Harding's well-known fathering of an illegitimate daughter. Is the unseen hand of the Duchess still at her home, continuing to defend the president's reputation? Some believe so.

Florence died on August 4, 1924, exactly a year and two days after her husband, but her story doesn't end with death. Some claim to have seen her stern face staring out the windows of her home-turned-museum late at night when the house is closed, locked, and supposedly empty. Florence's spirit may be as fiercely protective of her husband's reputation now as she was in life.

Unlike his wife's ghost, the phantom of Warren Harding does not interact with the living. His ghost allegedly shows up now and then at his Marion home, either in the living room or on the large front porch. Typically, he flashes the broad smile for which he was famous, and then he simply fades from sight. That smile won him the presidency. He was a compromise candidate, a dark horse who had been selected to break a stalemate. He had no enemies, having skillfully avoided stands on controversial issues. He did little to annoy anyone; his easygoing, friendly reassurance that he would preside over a low-key "return to normalcy," as he put it, earned him the White House. He is still smiling, or at least his ghost is. Just don't cross his wife. He seldom did.

# Calvin Coolidge

## 1872–1933
## 30th President, 1923–1929

Given Calvin Coolidge's famously dour, no-nonsense personality, it is not surprising that few claim to have seen his ghost. Doubtless, Coolidge's spirit shares the living man's strong work ethic and disdain for drama, a "let's get the work done without fuss" approach, with fondness for privacy.

Like Abraham Lincoln's son, Willie, Coolidge's son, Calvin Jr., died in the White House. Also like Lincoln, Coolidge was profoundly affected by his son's death. Coolidge's decision not to run for reelection in 1928 was strongly influenced by his son's tragic death. His son's ghost is said to still haunt the family's home in rural Vermont.

A seemingly out-of-place spirit is said to appear from time to time in the tiny village of Plymouth Notch. It is the phantom of a teenage boy dressed in tennis whites, shirt, shorts, socks, and shoes. The boy is limping noticeably. Who else could this be but Calvin Coolidge Jr.?

Everything about the village, now frozen in time exactly as it looked on August 3, 1923, is connected with the Coolidge family. On that date, Vice President Coolidge was sworn into office as the new president following the death of President Warren G. Harding. The oath of office was administered by the light of a kerosene lamp by the new president's father, a notary public and former sheriff.

The village was the boyhood home of the new president, who had been born across the street in the building that contained the general store. The entire village was donated to the state as a historic park by the president's older son, successful businessman and conservationist John Coolidge.

But why would the spirit of the younger son still appear in Plymouth Notch, and why is he in tennis clothes and limping? It is a sad story and one that determined the president's fate.

As in many families, the elder son was the heir to the father's driving ambition to do good and to do well. John was the serious, determined, and dedicated image of his father, while Calvin Jr. was more lighthearted, playful, and outgoing. He was a charmer in contrast to his notoriously tight-lipped father.

In common with many other presidential children, Coolidge's sons found the constant company of their Secret Service protectors to be a little annoying sometimes, and they didn't welcome the overbearing attention of crowds in public places. Thus, the family's frequent visits to remote Plymouth Notch represented relative freedom and quality time with doting relatives.

In the White House, with both his parents absorbed in official duties and his older brother away at university, Calvin Jr.'s retreat was the tennis court on the south lawn. He would play game after game until he was exhausted. During the summer of 1924, he developed a blister on his toe while playing tennis, but kept right on playing several more matches. Within hours, septicemia had set in. In the days before antibiotics, blood poisoning overcame him. He died on July 7. His father was stunned. All the privileges and powers of the presidency could not help save his son. The president later wrote, "He begged me to help him, but I could not. When he went, all the power and glory of the presidency went with him." Coolidge refused to run for reelection and returned to Plymouth Notch.

And so, Calvin Jr., still in his tennis whites, limps through the single street and surrounding fields of Plymouth Notch, remembering the good times. He is, in his father's words, "a boy for all eternity."

# Herbert Hoover

## 1874–1964
## 31st President, 1929–1933

Just looking at the expression on this phantom's face is enough to tell you whether the nation is at peace or at war. The questions of war and peace always were of prime importance to the living man and continue to concern his spirit. Ironically, the man's place in history has emphasized his perceived failures and not his considerable achievements. He'd hoped to be remembered as a man who consistently worked for peace, charity, and efficiency in government. Instead, his public image became that of an inept blunderer who couldn't seem to comprehend, much less cope with, an economic crisis. Meet the ghost of President Herbert Hoover.

Hoover's phantom takes the form of a rather rotund, balding, late-middle-aged man. He is wearing a very conservative three-piece, dark blue, pinstriped suit, and his round, fleshy face seldom bears a smile. His expression is either that of bland distraction, deep in thought, or more likely these days, deeply frowning at bad news. War, or the threat of war, is bad news indeed to Hoover, whose life was shaped by his concerns to aid the victims of war and try to prevent conflict.

His spirit is said to frequent the Hoover Tower, a prominent landmark on the campus of Stanford University in Palo Alto, California. The 285-foot-tall tower houses the Hoover Institution of War, Revolution, and Peace, a public-policy research center devoted to the study of world conflict. Hoover founded and endowed the institution in 1919, shortly after the end of World War I and some nine years before his election as president.

Orphaned at age nine, Hoover was big on self-reliance. His interest in fostering peace traces back to the influence of his mother, an ordained Quaker minister. He earned a degree in geology and mining engineering at Stanford. His work in developing mines took him to China, where he observed firsthand the poverty prevailing in underdeveloped countries. Hoover became a millionaire through his expertise and skillful money management. He had a reputation for being a superbly efficient manager, and President Woodrow Wilson asked him to organize American relief efforts in Europe. Hoover headed the Committee for Belgian Relief, the U.S. Food Administration for Europe, and the American Relief Administration.

As an engineer, Hoover understood how systems functioned. He saw the dilemma of feeding starving people as a problem of restoring old systems or creating new systems of food production, processing, and distribution. He identified new, alternative sources of food, oversaw development of processing plants, and created transportation systems to reach consumers. He was brilliantly successful and became an international hero.

His efforts at organizing food shipments probably saved millions of lives, and he became so popular that both political parties urged him to run for president in 1920. Hoover declined on the grounds that he needed experience in government, serving instead as secretary of commerce under presidents Warren Harding and Calvin Coolidge.

Hoover's background as an engineer made him a very different candidate for the presidency. Most presidents, before and since, had been lawyers or military professionals. Almost all had served in state legislatures, moving up to the U.S. Congress or state governorships. Astonishingly, Hoover had never run for public office before being nominated for the presidency. He won by a significant margin.

Unfortunately for Hoover and everyone else, his undoubted organizational skills were unable to affect a timely solution of the economic crisis of the Great Depression. The scale of the crisis was unprecedented; no one knew how to cope with it.

Hoover's presidency, from 1929 to 1933, is forever associated with the onset of the Great Depression. He was blamed, fairly or unfairly, for this economic and social disaster.

After his presidency, Hoover supported American policy on World War II, but became a vocal critic of the Cold War policy based on nuclear weapons. He returned to his longtime interest on preventing wars, and it seems that his spirit maintains his deep conviction that wars must be avoided if at all possible.

# Franklin D. Roosevelt

1882–1945
32nd President, 1933–1945

The ghosts of Franklin D. Roosevelt and his first lady, Eleanor, are said to have appeared at several different locations associated with their lives. Franklin and Eleanor's ghosts are interesting, all the more so because of their great historic significance. The most unusual ghost associated with the thirty-second president, however, is that of a close associate and honorary family member.

Franklin and Eleanor are buried side by side in the rose garden of Franklin's birthplace and family home at Hyde Park, New York. There is a third grave, less well-known to the world, nearby. It is the final resting place of Franklin's "court jester," the friend who provided many hearty laughs during challenging crises and difficult times. Though American born, this favorite companion was of Scotch ancestry. He came into Roosevelt's life in 1940, five years before the president's death, and seldom left his side during that time. He was a constant companion, traveling with Roosevelt throughout the United States; it was his total devotion to the president that earned him a grave up close to that of Roosevelt himself.

This particular ghost is heard more often than he is seen. His short, sharp barks have been heard in the rose garden, the Roosevelt home itself, and allegedly, at the "Little White House" in Warm Springs, Georgia. When this ghost materializes, it is in the form of a small black Scottish terrier with a bouncy walk and a perennially wagging tail. Meet the ghost of Fala.

Fala was born on April 7, 1940, and entered the White House by early summer, a gift to the president from his cousin. When

Fala arrived in the president's household, he had already been trained to lie down, sit up and beg, roll over, and politely scratch at the door when he needed to go outside. He was particularly good at begging, so much so that the White House staff would overfeed him with tasty treats and he would get sick. Fala starred in a 1943 documentary film about his role in the president's life. He became so popular that he was assigned his own secretary to answer his mail. Fala survived his master by seven years, dying just two days before his twelfth birthday. His spirit lives on, at least in the form of ghostly barks, at Hyde Park and Warm Springs.

At Roosevelt's getaway cottage at Warm Springs, visitors notice that the glass sidelights around the front door bear many little scratch marks, evidence of Fala's request to be let outside to "do his business." If scratching did not lead to an open door soon enough to suit the little dog, a sharp "woof" would be heard. There are those who swear that they've heard the scratching and the impatient woof at the door, only to turn and see nothing there. At least nothing from this world!

Incidentally, in life, Fala was well attuned to the spirit world. As noted elsewhere, he refused to enter the Lincoln bedroom. He was a very sociable creature, a real party animal who always joined cocktail parties, usually in hopes of conning visitors out of a canapé or two. He would not linger, however, at any gathering in the Yellow Room, site of other Lincoln ghost reports.

Roosevelt's ghost is alleged to have appeared in at least four venues—at Hyde Park, at his summer home on Campobello, in his Warm Springs cottage where he died, and aboard the presidential railcar, the Ferdinand Magellan.

The museum at the Roosevelt home at Hyde Park includes a replica of the president's White House office. The replica was actually used by Roosevelt when in residence at Hyde Park. The display features the president's homemade wheelchair, and this relic occasionally is occupied by the misty figure of Roosevelt, or so the story goes. Under the seat is a large red ashtray—the president was a heavy cigarette smoker. Some believe that they've seen wisps of smoke rising from the ashtray.

The Roosevelt summer "cottage" on Campobello Island in New Brunswick, Canada, is not small. Its thirty-four rooms include eighteen bedrooms intended to accommodate the Roosevelt's five children, visiting friends, and a large staff. It was at this cool summer retreat in August 1921 that the future president was stricken by polio, leaving him unable to walk for the rest of his life. His ghost, however, as manifested at Campobello is that of a vigorous man in a bathing suit, seen running, swimming, or sailing along with his active brood. Is his spirit reliving those last glorious, carefree days before the onset of paralysis in his legs? This happy vision is said to appear in August of every year.

There have only been a few reports of Roosevelt's spirit appearing at the scene of his death—his hideaway cottage at Warm Springs, Georgia. He had gone to Warm Springs in search of a cure for his disability. There was no cure, but he did feel better swimming in the naturally warm waters. He built a small cottage there before being elected president and died there of a cerebral hemorrhage on April 12, 1945, only one month into his fourth term in office. This rarely seen spirit is in the form of an exhausted and very sick old man.

Did the president, knowing that he would soon die, choose to spend his last days away from the White House and its ever-present press corps? A few speculate that Roosevelt did not want to die in the White House out of concern that doing so might somehow put a curse on the executive mansion. Roosevelt had many strong ties to the White House, which may have convinced him that he had been destined to become president. As a child, his father, an influential Democrat campaign contributor, took him to the White House to meet president Grover Cleveland. When young Franklin expressed an interest in becoming president, Cleveland is said to have cautioned him that it was indeed a difficult job—"a real killer." Franklin was a fourth cousin of Ulysses S. Grant and a fifth cousin of Theodore Roosevelt. When Franklin was invited to the White House by TR, he met the president's niece, Eleanor, his future wife.

Roosevelt's spirit is said to occasionally materialize in his presidential railroad car, the Ferdinand Magellan. Designated

U.S. Car Number One, the railcar has been retired and can be visited at the Gold Coast Railway Museum, located near the Miami Zoo in Dade County, Florida.

The Magellan had been built in 1922 by the Pullman Company, one of six luxurious private cars intended to be leased to millionaires. It was rebuilt and heavily armored in 1943 to meet the needs of President Roosevelt. The Secret Service felt that an armored railcar would be the safest means of moving Roosevelt around the country in wartime. In two years, Roosevelt put 50,000 miles on it. The car has four bedrooms, a full bath, a dining room–conference room, a kitchen and pantry, and a special wheelchair elevator, since removed.

The president's phantom is alleged to appear seated in the conference room. His figure is said to be almost transparent and trembling slightly. He is seen smoking a cigarette and studying papers.

The ghost of Eleanor Roosevelt is said to appear at her cottage, Val-Kill on the Hyde Park estate. Eleanor had Val-Kill built as a private retreat where she could relax away from her domineering mother-in-law, Sara. Eleanor was happiest entertaining her friends at Val-Kill, which she made her permanent home following her husband's death. Eleanor outlived Franklin by sixteen years, which included a stint as America's first delegate to the United Nations General Assembly. Her ghost is said to be quietly content, perhaps reflecting on a long life, full of accomplishments.

An interesting ghost associated with Franklin Roosevelt is that of his longtime lady friend, Lucy Mercer Rutherford. Lucy was such a frequent guest of the president that she was assigned her own code name, "Mrs. Johnson," by the Secret Service. Some local residents around a small northern New Jersey town swear that they have seen Lucy's ghost waiting patiently at the now-disused train station, peering into the growing dusk, waiting for her lover's train to arrive, as it often did during his later life. It is certain that she appreciated the gallant gesture of her one true love in coming to visit her, for he had much to lose if their continuing love affair had become known.

Lucy had been born to a socially prominent but impoverished family. Well-educated and with a charming, poised personality, the beautiful young woman worked for $25 a week as the social secretary to Eleanor Roosevelt. She quickly caught Franklin's attention. Soon, Lucy was registering at secluded hotels as her lover's "wife" and an intense love affair had begun.

Franklin was very reluctant to leave his wife and five children. Lucy was well aware that her first and greatest love was offered a divorce by his outraged wife when she learned of the affair, but his mother had threatened to cut her only son off without a penny if he ended the marriage. The wife and mother both demanded that the affair with the lovely social secretary end permanently.

Lucy found another job, as governess to a wealthy New Jersey widower with five children to raise. She soon married her employer, Winthrop Rutherford, who at age fifty-eight was exactly twice Lucy's age of twenty-nine. When her husband died in his old age, Lucy became very wealthy, richer by far than her true love.

Their relationship flourished in secrecy for the rest of Roosevelt's life. They met whenever his wife was out of town, which fortunately for the lovers was frequent. After Lucy Rutherford was widowed, President Roosevelt made a habit of detouring to visit her in her north Jersey home when on his way from his office to weekend visits to his Hyde Park home in New York's Hudson Valley.

Lucy really looked forward to those occasions when her longtime lover's train stopped just for him and her. It was a spectacular as well as joyous time when the Ferdinand Magellan pulled slowly into the little whistle-stop station for another secret rendezvous.

Lucy's ghost still visits the trackside where the most important man in the world at the time stopped just to spend a few hours with her in her country home. No wonder her spirit still occasionally peers down the track, anticipating another meeting.

# Harry S. Truman

## 1884–1972
## 33rd President, 1945–1953

The small cloud of mist gradually takes recognizable form, almost as if solidifying or coming into sharper focus. The faint image is that of a man of medium height, about sixty, and wearing eyeglasses with round lenses and metal frames. As the ghostly image becomes clearer and brighter, it becomes apparent that the man is wearing a brightly colored, short-sleeved shirt in a bold floral print. The tanned face breaks into a broad smile, and then abruptly the man is gone. It is as though he was evaporated in the bright sunshine of Key West, Florida. Those who have caught a quick glimpse of this phantom are lucky indeed, for they have seen the ghost of President Harry S. Truman.

Why this Missourian who became president on the sudden death of his predecessor, Franklin D. Roosevelt, would appear with some regularity at Key West is an interesting story. His favorite retreat, now known as the Truman Cottage, is a modest, converted old barracks on the grounds of the former naval air station in Key West. Truman, like most other presidents, looked forward to brief respites from the ceremonial restraints and pressure cooker atmosphere of the White House. "The great white jail" was Truman's name for it, and he needed to put distance, both geographical and psychological distance, between himself and the capital.

President Roosevelt had created a rustic retreat in Maryland's Catoctin Mountains, later named Camp David by Dwight D. Eisenhower. Truman decided that he wanted a tropical environment, especially in winter. He had little money and couldn't afford to purchase a vacation home in Florida. Neither did he want the government to spend a lot of money on a suitable

"Little White House." He was always frugal with government money and had made his reputation in the Senate as the head of a wartime commission charged with eliminating waste in government contracts.

The perfect solution was the guest cottage, comfortable but not pretentious, at Key West's naval station. Built in 1890, William Howard Taft had visited it briefly. Inventor Thomas Edison stayed there for six months while working on new weapons for the Navy. It would cost the government nothing to let the president use it. Truman made eleven trips to Key West, spending a total of 175 days in its winter sunshine, and always wearing flamboyant Hawaiian sports shirts to emphasize the vacation mood. And so he returned, at least in spirit, to the place where he was most relaxed during an eventful and stressful presidency. His cottage is now open to the public.

Truman's spirit is said to make very rare appearances at his birthplace in Lamar, Missouri. He was born in a very small, 20-by-28-foot house, which his parents had bought for $685 two years earlier. At the time, the house lacked both indoor plumbing and electricity.

In 1959, the United Auto Workers donated the house to the state of Missouri to be preserved as a historic site. The former president attended the dedication ceremony when he was seventy-five years old. It is this elderly figure that has been seen as a spirit, nostalgically admiring the little house from which he traveled so far.

Another equally rare venue for Truman's ghost is said to be in the exact replica of his oval office within the Harry S. Truman Library and Museum in Independence, Missouri. Perhaps Truman's spirit feels comfortable in such familiar surroundings, where he made so many momentous and highly controversial decisions. This oval office phantom may be taking some quiet satisfaction in the fact that most historians would now rate him among the nation's best presidents, a nice change from the dismal approval rating of twenty-two percent when he left office. His ghost wears a faint smile. Harry did it his way, and he was right.

# Dwight D. Eisenhower

## 1890–1969
## 34th President, 1953–1961

Is the ghost of Dwight D. Eisenhower trying to tell us something? Those who reportedly have seen the phantom of the nation's thirty-fourth chief executive think so. According to reports, the faintly phosphorescent figure, seated at his desk, is described as gazing speculatively upward, as though pondering the skies, an expression of awe and anxiety on his face. Is the onetime five-star general's ghost still expressing concern about a rather startling event that supposedly captured his full attention in early 1954? There have been persistent rumors that Eisenhower had been shown hard evidence of an alien spacecraft, during a secret visit to Edwards Air Force Base in Southern California.

The term UFO was coined in the post–World War II period when a flurry of supposed sightings captured public attention. The government has consistently denied that any irrefutable evidence of alien spacecraft has ever been found. Reported sightings of UFOs routinely are dismissed as cases of mistaken identity or unbelievable witnesses, yet several U.S. presidents claim to have seen UFOs. Highly trained observers, including astronauts and military and civilian pilots, have reported encounters with unknown aircraft possessing stunning speed and unprecedented maneuverability.

Before entering the White House, California governor Ronald Reagan was returning to his state capital in a private plane. His plane was approached by a UFO, which shadowed the governor's craft. Reagan ordered his pilot to pursue the stranger, but it proved much too fast to follow. Jimmy Carter once filed an official report of an encounter with a UFO. These presidents have a lot of company in their beliefs in UFOs and the possibility of visits by extraterrestrial life forms.

A 1996 Gallup poll found that seventy-two percent of Americans think that there is life on other planets in the universe. Twenty-two percent think that these intelligent life forms have made contact with us. Interestingly, seventy-one percent believe that the U.S. government knows more about UFOs than it is telling.

These figures were noted in a June 19, 1997, article by Richard Price, which appeared in *USA Today*. His article focused on a UFO event near Phoenix on March 13 of that year, which was witnessed by thousands of people, including the governor of Arizona, who was a trained, experienced pilot.

Governor Fife Symington was flying in toward Sky Harbor Airport when he saw an "enormous" craft in the sky. The mysterious craft was performing high-speed maneuvers far beyond the capabilities of known aircraft. Symington, then in his second term as governor, kept quiet about the experience out of his concern that his report might cause widespread alarm. He later commented, as reported in the Tucson *Arizona Daily Star* of March 23, that "the universe is a big place and we're conceited to think that we're alone."

President Eisenhower never discussed UFOs, at least not in any public record. Many believe, however, that he made a top-secret visit to Edwards Air Force Base on Saturday, February 20, 1954, for a briefing on UFOs. Some allege that he was shown wreckage and possibly bodies from a UFO. It is known that the president and his first lady, Mamie, were vacationing in nearby Palm Springs from February 17 to February 24. On the evening of February 20, Eisenhower "disappeared" from the official records that track his whereabouts and activities. Official logs show no visitors or meetings and no incoming or outgoing phone calls, unusual for presidents even when on vacation. Just what did the president do during the hours when he "went missing" from official diaries and logs? Did he learn something about UFOs? His ghost, it is said, still sits in his den at his Gettysburg home, looking heavenward, still keeping a potentially awesome secret.

The ghosts of Dwight and Mamie Eisenhower are drawn back to their Gettysburg farm for an excellent reason. This was where, in life, they were most at peace. The remodeled farmhouse on the western edge of the Gettysburg battlefield was the first and only home they ever owned. As Mamie said on many occasions, "We had only one home, our farm." They bought the 189-acre farm in 1950, after thirty-four years of married life spent in military housing. Mamie calculated that she and Ike had lived in thirty-seven residences, mostly on Army posts, before buying their first home.

The Eisenhowers already were familiar with the Gettysburg area. The future president had studied the terrain of the battlefield as part of his military training and had been stationed at Camp Colt, located on land once the site of Pickett's Charge. They purchased a somewhat dilapidated one-hundred-year-old farmhouse and set about renovating it into a twenty-room Georgian Revival mansion. They soon discovered a two-hundred-year-old log cabin hidden inside the house. Unfortunately, termites had also discovered the log cabin, little of which could be salvaged. The president's study or den is located within this oldest part of the structure; it may be that these ancient timbers retain some of the psychic energy of long-ago occupants.

Curiously, Mamie's spirit has been seen, and heard, much more often than that of Ike, whose shade appears only occasionally in his den and in the living room, where he had informal talks with world leaders like Winston Churchill, Nikita Khrushchev, and Charles de Gaulle. The living room, like the den, was Ike's turf, and his spirit is still there. In contrast, Mamie's domain was the sun porch and her large bedroom.

Mamie's greatest luxury was to stay in bed all morning, writing letters and phoning family and friends. "No public appearances before noon!" was her seldom-broken rule. During weekend visits in the White House years and afterward in retirement, Mamie liked to have lunch served on trays on the sunroom while watching television. She admitted to being addicted to several soap operas; her misty form has been spotted both in the sunroom and her bedroom. The heavy, mirrored doors of her clothes closet can be heard opening and closing when no one is in her room, and mysterious footsteps are heard on the second floor.

The living room contains a large, illuminated curio cabinet. In it, Mamie displayed an eclectic mix of little souvenirs from their travels, valuable gifts from foreign governments, dime-store gewgaws, gifts from ordinary citizens, and handcrafted items from her grandchildren. If it was a gift, Mamie displayed it, regardless of its intrinsic value. Once, long after Mamie's death, a park service employee cleaned and dusted the collection, replacing the items differently than the original arrangement. Reportedly, the tiny figures and souvenirs had been restored to their original positions by the next morning. You don't mess with Mamie's collections.

Eisenhower enjoyed only eight years of retirement at his Gettysburg farm; he died in 1969 of congestive heart failure. Mamie lived on for an additional ten years before her fatal stroke. She spent much of those lonely years in her second-floor bedroom suite. Some say her spirit is still in the bedroom. Some visitors claim to hear a rustling or crinkling sound and sense an unseen person brushing past them. Are they hearing the faint sounds of Mamie's taffeta dress, her favorite material? The pleasant odor of Mamie's favorite floral perfume can sometimes be detected in her bedroom. The perfume bottles still on display in her room were found, however, to be tightly sealed.

Once, a psychic took the usual house tour available to tourists but claimed to have been contacted by Mamie's spirit. The psychic reported to the National Park Service that Mamie was concerned that the back stairs, used as the tour exit, were in need of repair. The skeptical park service investigated and necessary repairs were made. Several guests at the house claim to have seen a window shade in Mamie's room slowly raise and then lower as they were leaving the property after the last tour of the day. Many staff and visitors believe that the Eisenhowers never really left their dream home, at least in spirit.

# John F. Kennedy

## 1917–1963
## 35th President, 1961–1963

There is an impressive list of tragedies that have befallen the Kennedy family. It is believed by some that this is the result of a curse alleged to have originated back in Ireland after a bitter argument over a land deal gone sour. Was the bad luck that struck John F. Kennedy's generation, continuing into the next, just coincidence, or was there, as Ted Kennedy speculated, a real curse operating? Out of the four sons of Joseph and Rose Kennedy, only Ted made it to old age. Joe Jr. died when his bomber exploded over the English Channel during World War II. Both John and Robert were murdered by assassins. Their mentally underdeveloped sister Rosemary was lobotomized in a misguided attempt to help her achieve a normal life. Sister Kathleen died in a plane crash. John's second son, Patrick, was born six weeks prematurely and lived only two days. John Jr. died in the crash of his private plane. This chain of disasters has convinced all but the most skeptical of the reality of a Kennedy family curse.

And then there is the zero-year curse, sometimes called Tenskwatawa's curse. This alleged curse goes back to 1811 and the Battle of Tippecanoe. Territorial Governor William Henry Harrison led American troops into a fierce battle against the Shawnee Indians, led by Chief Tecumseh. Although Harrison lost more men than Tecumseh, the Shawnee were resoundingly defeated.

Tecumseh's younger brother, Tenskwatawa, was a medicine man known as a prophet, because of his uncanny visions of the future and his supernatural powers. Following the Shawnee defeat at Tippecanoe he allegedly said, "The children of the land [the Shawnee] have risen against the white men and been struck down. Now the land itself will rise up, trembling like a wounded beast." Only months after the Battle of Tippecanoe, a massive earthquake struck the Mississippi Valley. Scientists now believe it was a stronger quake than that in San Francisco in 1906. The Mississippi and Ohio rivers actually reversed their flows temporarily. Dust blocked out the sun for days. A meadow suddenly sank fifteen feet or more, becoming a large lake, Reelfoot Lake, which is still there. This disastrous quake occurred on December 16, 1811, and was followed by two more massive quakes on January 20 and February 7, 1812, along with thousands of minor quakes.

Understandably, people began to take Tenskwatawa very seriously. When he heard that his old foe Harrison was running for president, Tenskwatawa predicted that the victor of Tippecanoe would not live out his term. "But no U.S. president has ever died in office," said the skeptics. "Harrison will die!" thundered Tenskwatawa, "and every twenty years afterward, the president elected in years ending in zero will die in office."

Harrison, elected in 1840, died after only a month in office. Lincoln, elected in 1860, was assassinated. Garfield, elected in 1880, and McKinley, reelected in 1900, were assassinated. Harding, elected in 1920, died in office. Roosevelt, reelected in 1940, died in office. Kennedy, elected in 1960, was assassinated.

Reagan, elected in 1980, was nearly killed by a would-be assassin, and some credit his miraculous survival to the psychic powers invoked by Nancy Reagan's many séances and confidence in astrologers. Perhaps Reagan's narrow escape marked the end of Tenskwatawa's zero-year curse. George W. Bush was elected twenty years later in 2000 and went on to complete that term and then another.

Many people interested in the paranormal have pointed out the eerie similarities and macabre coincidences between the assassinations of presidents Lincoln and Kennedy. Was it somehow written in the stars that Kennedy, elected exactly a century after Lincoln, should suffer the same fate? Both presidents were shot on a Friday, killed by a bullet fired into the back of the head, slain while seated next to their wives, in mourning for sons who died during their presidency, shot by southerners, and succeeded by southerners both named Johnson. Lincoln was first elected to Congress in 1846; Kennedy was first elected to Congress in 1946. Lincoln failed to win a vice presidential nomination in 1856; Kennedy failed to get a vice presidential nomination in 1956. In their elections, Lincoln defeated Stephen Douglas, born in 1813; Kennedy defeated Richard Nixon, born in 1913. Lincoln's secretary was named Kennedy; Kennedy's secretary was named Lincoln. Lincoln's assassin fired the fatal bullet in a theater and was captured in a warehouse; Kennedy's assassin fired from a warehouse and was captured in a theater. Neither assassin lived to be placed on trial.

Many people have reported seeing a bright, luminous mist over Kennedy's grave in Arlington National Cemetery. This mysterious mist is said to appear briefly at both dawn and dusk. A few claim to have seen Kennedy's figure near his grave just after the coffin was moved a short distance from the original site in order to install a permanent gas line to the eternal flame atop the grave; the first flame has been supplied from a buried propane tank. The necessary disturbance of the grave could have aroused his ghost.

Robert Kennedy selected the grave site, on the slope of a hill below the Lee Mansion, overlooking the Potomac River and the city of Washington. He said that the view was so impressive that he could spend a lot of time there. Following his assassination in 1968, Robert was buried near his brother. The view is still impressive.

The three-and-a-half-acre grave site now includes the final resting places of Kennedy, his widow Jacqueline, his brothers Robert and Ted, and two infants, Patrick and an unnamed stillborn daughter. Millions of people have paid their respects at the grave; as many as three thousand per hour have filed past.

Both Kennedy and his wife are thought to have believed in some form of existence after death. It is known that Jackie Kennedy wrote a letter to her dead husband and had it placed in his coffin. She may have continued to write him letters until her own death.

A few visitors to Kennedy's boyhood home believe that they've sensed a presence there. The birthplace is a modest frame house in the Boston suburb of Brookline. It was the first home shared by the president's parents, Joe and Rose. After Kennedy's death, the family repurchased and restored the house to its appearance during John's boyhood. Donated to the National Park Service, the house offers the ambiance, if not the ghost, of the thirty-fifth president.

Perhaps the most profoundly tragic ghost associated with Kennedy is that of his widow, whose great dignity and grace helped a mourning nation through the funeral. Dayton, Ohio, Wilbur and Orville Wright's hometown, is the site of the National Museum of the U.S. Air Force. The museum's Presidential Aircraft Gallery enables tourists to visit the planes that served presidents Franklin D. Roosevelt, Harry S. Truman, John F. Kennedy, and Lyndon B. Johnson. One particular Air Force One, a Boeing 707, holds a unique position within the presidential lineup, for it was the scene of the swearing in of the new president, Johnson, following the brutal assassination of his predecessor, whose corpse then was carried back to Washington in the rear compartment. Some believe that this aircraft is haunted, though the ghost's appearances are not widely known, because most witnesses feel protective of this tragic spirit.

Only a handful of individuals have observed the phantom of Jackie, for she seems to possess the reserved dignity so characteristic of the living person. The very few willing to admit to seeing this spirit say that she appears only briefly as a barely visible, faintly shimmering mist. Her grief is so overwhelmingly evident in her dejected posture, downcast eyes, and utterly desolate expression that observers instinctively look away in profound sympathy.

# Lyndon B. Johnson

## 1908–1973
## 36th President, 1963–1969

The ghostly appearances of Lyndon B. Johnson occur within a tightly circumscribed area centered on Johnson City, a settlement founded by his grandparents. Within just thirteen miles of beautiful Texas hill country, Johnson was born, raised, and educated. Here, he purchased the ranch that became his "Western White House." And there he was buried. It has been said of many people that in order to understand them, one must understand their personal geography, the land that gave them their identity. This close relationship of the man and his land is nowhere more evident than in Johnson's life, and perhaps his afterlife.

"Home" is a very powerful concept. Patriotism rests on the foundation of a homeland, a piece of the earth with which one has a special, almost mystical bond. One's home, in a broad sense, provides emotional support and encouragement—something well understood by athletes, who on the average perform better on their home fields.

Many Americans are highly mobile in their lifetimes. They are likely to be born, grow up, attend college, and start their careers in different communities, even different states. Promotions, changes in jobs, or career shifts may take them to yet more locations, followed eventually by retirement to another distant place. But none of this was true for Johnson, or LBJ as he liked to be known. LBJ had strong roots in Johnson City and the surrounding ranchlands. His roots sustained him through his very active, sometimes turbulent career. There can be no surprise that his ghost is said to appear where his heart lay—at his ranch, his boyhood home, and his grave site.

LBJ was said to be a classic Type A personality, hard driving, hard working, and hard playing. At six feet, three inches, he seemed larger than life. And he was full of life, always thinking and doing and always in motion. During his five years in the White House, he returned to his beloved 360-acre ranch as often as possible. An airstrip large enough for the presidential jet was built and equipped with the latest navigational aids so Johnson could be flown directly to his home. He always invited staff, associates, and political supporters along, where they found themselves working longer and harder than ever, interspersed with steak barbecues and guided tours of the ranch. Johnson was notorious for his high-speed tours in his big convertible, driven with reckless enthusiasm. There are those who claim to have seen his phantom convertible barreling over the distant meadows.

Given his hyper personality and lifestyle—three packs of cigarettes a day and scotch whiskey highballs—it is not surprising that LBJ died at his ranch of a heart attack. The fatal attack was his third. He is buried near his ranch house. The grave site, it is claimed, often features a strange, glowing mist, especially near dusk. Is the spirit of Lyndon Johnson still enjoying his special place, his home country that gave him so much emotional strength in his lifetime? It certainly would be appropriate.

# Richard Nixon

## 1913–1994
## 37th President, 1969–1974

There is a rumor, persistent but unverifiable, that Richard Nixon's ghost haunts the White House. While the White House is widely believed to hold many ghosts, Nixon's spirit might at first seem an unlikely candidate for such a haunting. While the venerable executive mansion was the scene of Nixon's many triumphs, it also was the scene of his fateful decision to attempt a cover-up of the infamous break-in of Democratic campaign headquarters at Watergate. That notorious obstruction of justice led to Nixon's tragic distinction as the only U.S. president ever to resign. Why would Nixon's spirit be drawn back to the site of his humiliation?

All U.S. presidents have had to cope with enormous pressures of leadership while in the White House; difficult and complex decisions are part of the daily routine. The burdens of office were, at least in Nixon's case, hugely magnified by his own bad decisions concerning the Watergate affair. Is Nixon's spirit endlessly reliving the bitter torment of his last days in the White House? Some people believe so.

It might seem more logical, if ghosts can be expected to behave logically, that Nixon, of all presidents, would choose not to return to the scene of his gut-wrenching agony, his protracted struggle to save his presidency and his reputation from the final surrender of resignation. Harry S. Truman, a skeptic who nonetheless believed that Lincoln's ghost roamed the halls of the White House, once commented, "Why would they want to come back here? I could never understand. No man in his right mind would want to come here of his own accord."

But what if Nixon's ghost has returned to the White House not out of true choice but by irresistible compulsion? All presidents are students of history. They are profoundly conscious of their role in making history. And, to a man, they each have been deeply concerned with how history will view them and their accomplishments.

Little is known about Nixon's beliefs in life after death or the spirit world. Like most politicians, he had become skilled in avoiding stands on controversial issues. Several credible eyewitnesses from the grim and traumatic days preceding Nixon's resignation, however, testify that the president may have suffered from some sort of nervous exhaustion or emotional breakdown. Secretary of State Henry Kissinger and Nixon's son-in-law

Edward Cox both observed a distraught president roaming the halls, pausing before the portraits of earlier presidents. Was Nixon trying to commune with the spirits of his predecessors? Some say that Nixon actually spoke to the paintings, seeking their advice on his dilemma. He is believed to have made particularly sincere attempts to reach out to the spirits of Lincoln and Theodore Roosevelt. Nixon much admired Lincoln's ability to function under enormous stress and Roosevelt's courage under fire. Nixon's spirit still may prowl the midnight halls of the White House, eternally seeking guidance from earlier presidents.

If the Nixon ghost allegedly stalking through the White House is the personification of anxiety, the version that reportedly haunts his birthplace in Yorba Linda, California, is more relaxed and reflective. This version of Nixon's spirit may reflect his post-presidential character. If it is true that extreme adversity reveals a person's true character, then the trauma of forced resignation spotlighted Nixon's positive energies. Following a near-death experience when a blood clot traveled from his phlebitis-swollen leg to his lung, Nixon embarked on a new career as an author. His immediate motivation was to pay his bills. Never a wealthy man, Nixon faced staggering legal bills. His long-range goal was to rehabilitate his tarnished reputation by demonstrating his deep understanding of global politics. He wrote ten books, all of them bestsellers and critical successes. By sheer willpower and hard work, Nixon changed his image from disgraced former president to respected elder statesman. Recent historians and political analysts have upgraded his rank among American presidents, emphasizing his impressive handling of foreign policy. No wonder that his Yorba Linda spirit is quietly reflective and mellow. His misty, almost translucent form is said to appear on occasion in the Richard Nixon Library and Museum's exact replica of the East Room of the White House.

Another ghost at Yorba Linda is seldom seen, and even when it is, the sighting is typically so brief that the observers aren't sure that they saw anything more than a fleeting shadow. This elusive phantom is the ghost of Nixon's first lady, Patricia.

In life, Pat Nixon was quite shy and self-effacing. She appeared to be somewhat uncomfortable in large crowds, although reportedly she was the picture of relaxed charm in smaller groups. Like other first ladies, such as Bess Truman, who did not seek out publicity, Pat was underestimated. Despite her shy demeanor, she set new records in the number of people she invited to the White House. She supported volunteerism during her time as first lady and even traveled to Vietnam to visit American troops.

Pat was born Thelma Catherine Ryan on March 16, 1912. Her Irish-American father joked that she just missed being his St. Patrick's Day present and nicknamed her Pat. She changed her name legally to Patricia as an adult. She worked as a movie extra to help pay her way through college, graduating with honors from the University of Southern California in 1937. It was while teaching high school in Whittier that Pat met an ambitious young lawyer named Richard Nixon. He proposed on the first date. Pat waited two years before saying yes.

Pat died ten months before her husband, in June 1993, and was buried at the Richard Nixon Library and Museum in Yorba Linda. Her spirit has been briefly glimpsed in the gardens adjoining her burial plot, enjoying the beauty and tranquility of the rosebushes.

It is said that frequently people subconsciously choose mates whose character traits balance or contrast with their own. Nixon definitely was a hard-driving Type A personality. In Pat, Nixon found a smart, hardworking partner, but one with a calm, balanced, and controlled persona. Perhaps it is not at all surprising that Pat's spirit takes the time to smell the roses.

# Gerald Ford

## 1913–2006
## 38th President, 1974–1977

Is it a recurring technological malfunction, frequent cases of overactive imaginations on the part of visitors, or a supernatural occurrence? No one seems really sure, but it does seem to happen. Visitors to the Gerald R. Ford Presidential Library and Museum in Grand Rapids, Michigan, swear they've seen it. Visitors to the museum can take a high-tech holographic tour of Ford's White House. Many reportedly have seen a human-shaped shadow cross their field of vision repeatedly during the tour, a shadow that looks a lot like Gerald Ford. And yet, no persons are supposed to be seen on the electronic tour. Did the cameras unintentionally pick up the psychic energies of Ford's spirit?

So-called "spirit photographs," pictures alleged to reveal the ghosts or spirits of the dead, have been around since the earliest days of photography. Many are obvious frauds or deliberate or accidental double exposures, such as the famous spirit photograph of the widowed Mary Todd Lincoln with her deceased husband standing behind her. But what about those which cannot be dismissed as frauds? As Rosemary Ellen Guiley writes in *The Encyclopedia of Ghosts and Spirits*, the Ghost Research Society of Oak Lawn, Illinois, analyzes spirit photographs. About ninety percent of alleged supernatural images can be explained naturally—flaws in film, flaws in developing, or random patterns of shadows or reflections. But that leaves ten percent unexplained. Is it merely a product of overactive imaginations on the part of some viewers that fleeting, vaguely misty images appear in the holographic tour of Ford's White House? You might want to see for yourself.

With or without possible paranormal images, a visit to Ford's Presidential Museum will be interesting. Most historians now agree that Ford—strong, steady, unpretentious, and eminently decent—was the right man to take over following the trauma of the Watergate crisis. His straightforward honesty and integrity "helped the nation to heal" in President Jimmy Carter's words. Contrary to the clumsy image resulting from a few on-camera stumbles, Ford was an accomplished athlete. An all-star football player, he turned down an opportunity to play pro ball, and he excelled at skiing, golf, and tennis. An unassuming man, he once commented wryly that "he was a Ford, not a Lincoln."

Ford's birthplace was torn down in 1971 following a fire. The site has been marked by a memorial and rose garden. There, at 3202 Woolworth Avenue in Omaha, Nebraska, some visitors smell aromatic pipe tobacco, although no apparition appears. Ford did smoke about eight bowlfuls of tobacco a day. Apparently his ghost does too. Visit the birthsite and smell for yourself.

# Jimmy Carter

## 1924–
## 39th President, 1977–1981

Successful political leaders have learned to avoid public comment on any and all paranormal or supernatural phenomena. Perhaps the over-the-top media firestorm precipitated by Nancy Reagan's contacts with astrologers has made them extra cautious about revealing their thoughts on these topics. Even a casual joke about ghosts can produce a frenzy of mocking criticism.

Jimmy Carter is alone among the living ex-presidents in risking the adverse publicity that seems to follow any mention of controversial experiences or thoughts. Only Carter and Ronald Reagan have admitted seeing UFOs, and only Carter has mentioned, however skeptically, an experience in a possibly haunted house. In his book, *An Hour before Daylight: Memories of a Rural Boyhood*, Carter mentions the haunted house in his neighborhood. Concerning this house, "There were frequent reports of a woman who could be seen through the attic windows, wearing a long white flowing dress and carrying a candle, apparently looking for something or someone she had lost. . . . I really tried to discount these kinds of tales, but I sometimes thought I had glimpses of the searching woman, which may have been a reflection of the setting sun or Venus in the western window." Carter then relates a personal experience when he was in that same house while helping to care for its dying owner, a medical doctor. Late one night, he heard the doctor's dogs begin a weird howling. He and an attending nurse rushed into the bedroom, discovering that the doctor had just died. "We assumed that the dogs had seen his spirit leaving the house."

Oddly enough, Jimmy and his wife Rosalynn later lived in that same house between 1956 and 1960. In an interview with *Good Housekeeping* magazine, as quoted in Joel Martin and William Birnes' *The Haunting of the Presidents,* Rosalynn said, "I knew about the ghost before Jimmy and I moved in, but I wasn't really afraid of it. I just never disturbed it by going into the 'haunted room' alone at night."

A woman who had worked as a cook in the house before the Carters reported, "I'd see a woman with a long white dress coming from the cemetery. Dr. Wise, the man I worked for, could see her too. He'd say it was our imaginations, but when he spoke to the woman, she and the light she carried both vanished."

Was Carter's willingness to live in a house reputed to be haunted a sign of profound skepticism about ghosts or an example of great courage? Perhaps we'll never really know, but Carter deserves credit for his straightforward discussion of possible paranormal experiences.

# Ronald Reagan

## 1911–2004
## 40th President, 1981–1989

The ghost of Ronald Reagan has so far been elusive, seeming to appear very briefly only on rare occasions. There are persistent, though unsubstantiated, rumors that the ghost of one of America's most popular presidents has appeared several times at his beloved ranch home, Rancho del Cielo. If indeed Reagan's spirit has chosen to return to his ranch, it is an entirely appropriate and predictable venue, for this was his favorite place on earth.

Reagan felt most at home on the 688-acre ranch that he and his wife Nancy purchased in 1974. In keeping with his love of horseback riding, the Reagans had owned ranches before, but they fell in love with this one the first time they saw it. The new name they chose, which translates as "Ranch of Heaven," says it all. "It may not be heaven exactly," Reagan joked, "but it's in the same zip code." The ranch, now owned by the Ronald Reagan and Young America Foundation, is maintained as a tribute to the former president.

During his eight-year presidency, Reagan frequently visited his "Western White House" in order to, as he put it, "recharge his batteries." It has been estimated that, all told, he spent one year of his presidency at his ranch. As an experienced actor, he knew the value of the star being offstage for a while; his return to center stage would be all the more anticipated and welcomed. Similarly, his spirit is not frequently in evidence.

In life, Reagan made few public comments on the paranormal, but his wife Nancy's interest in astrology became the subject of public controversy. In a book by former White House chief of staff Donald Regan, published in 1988, it was alleged that an astrologer helped plan the president's schedule.

Allegedly, Nancy consulted astrologers concerning avoidance of dangerous times for being out in public or scheduling key meetings. Although all occupants of the White House, at least in recent years, have been subjected to intense scrutiny and criticism, Nancy Reagan seems to have been subjected to truly vicious attacks, in particular in regards to her contacts with astrologers. She was quoted in *America's First Ladies*, lamenting, "I sometimes had the feeling that if it was raining outside, it was probably my fault. . . . Based on the press reports I read . . . I wouldn't have liked me either." Her heartfelt advice to future first ladies: "Once you're in the White House, don't think it's going to be a glamorous, fairy-tale life. It's very hard work with high highs and low lows. Since you're under a microscope, everything is magnified, so just keep your perspective and your patience."

Was Reagan's official schedule influenced by astrology? It is curious that his first swearing-in as California's governor took place at six minutes past midnight. It was observed that Air Force One departures took place either twenty minutes before or twenty minutes after the hour, never on the hour. In her 1989 book *My Turn*, Nancy wrote that "astrology was simply one of the ways I coped with the fear I felt after my husband almost died" in 1981. The would-be assassin's bullet penetrated to less than an inch from the president's heart, enough to suggest extreme caution to his loving wife. According to Joel Martin and William Birnes in the book, *The Haunting of the Presidents*, Nancy was very much aware of the twenty-year death curse of Tenskwatawa.

Does the spirit of Reagan make very private contacts with the love of his life, his adoring wife? In an 2009 interview with a writer from *Vanity Fair* magazine, Nancy is quoted as saying, "At nighttime, if I wake up, I think Ronnie is there and I start to talk to him . . . and I see him." Nancy has a lot of company in this experience. In a 1987 survey conducted by the University of Chicago's National Opinion Research Council, forty-two percent of adult Americans reported contact with deceased loved ones.

Sixty-seven percent of widows believed that their husband's spirits had made contact. Of these, seventy-eight percent saw an apparition, fifty percent heard one, and thirty-two percent felt a presence.

# Bibliography

## BOOKS

Adler, Bill, ed. *America's First Ladies*. Lanham, MD: Taylor Trade, 2002.

Alexander, John. *Ghosts: Washington's Most Famous Ghost Stories*. Washington, DC: Washingtonian Books, 1975.

Beckley, Timothy. *The UFO Silencers*. New Brunswick, NJ: Inner Light, 1990.

Bishop, Jim. *FDR's Last Year*. New York: Morrow, 1974.

Brown, Alan. *Haunted Tennessee: Ghosts and Strange Phenomena of the Volunteer State*. Mechanicsburg, PA: Stackpole Books, 2009.

Carter, Jimmy. *An Hour before Daylight*. New York: Simon and Schuster, 2001.

Clark, Jerome. *Unexplained!* Canton, MI: Visible Ink Press, 1999.

Coleman, Loren. *Mysterious America*. London: Faber and Faber, 1983.

DeGregorio, William. *The Complete Book of U.S. Presidents*. New York: Gramercy Books, 2001.

Epting, Chris. *The Birthplace Book: A Guide to Birth Sites of Famous People, Places, and Things*. Mechanicsburg, PA: Stackpole Books, 2009.

Garrison, Webb, and Beth Wieder. *A Treasury of White House Tales*. Nashville: Thomas Nelson, 2002.

Guiley, Rosemary Ellen. *The Encyclopedia of Ghosts and Spirits*. New York: Facts on File, 1992.

Hauck, Dennis. *Haunted Places: The National Directory*. New York: Penguin Putnam, 2002.

Hay, Peter. *All the Presidents' Ladies: Anecdotes of the Women behind the Men in the White House*. New York: Viking, 1988.

Krantz, Les. *America by the Numbers: Facts and Figures from the Weighty to the Way-Out*. Boston: Houghton Mifflin, 1993.

Lewis, David, and Darly Hicks. *The Presidential Zero Year Mystery*. Plainfield, NJ: Haven Books, 1980.

Martin, Joel, and William Birnes. *The Haunting of the Presidents*. New York: Signet, 2003.

Myes, Arthur. *The Ghostly Register*. New York: McGraw-Hill, 1986.

Nesbitt, Mark, and Patty A. Wilson. *The Big Book of Pennsylvania Ghost Stories*. Mechanicsburg, PA: Stackpole Books, 2008.

Norman, Michael, and Beth Scott. *Haunted America*. New York: Tom Doherty Associates, 1994.

Palette, Luann, and Fred Worth. *The World Almanac of Presidential Facts*. New York: World Almanac, 1988.

Parks, Lillian. *My Thirty Years Backstairs at the White House*. New York: Fleet, 1961.

Pickering, David. *Cassell Dictionary of Superstitions*. London: Cassell, 1995.

Reagan, Nancy. *My Turn: The Memoirs of Nancy Reagan*. New York: Random House, 1989.

Regan, Donald. *For the Record*. New York: Harcourt-Brace Jovanovich, 1988.

Seale, William. *The President's House*. Washington, DC: White House Historic Association, 1986.

Skinner, Charles. *American Myths and Legends*. Detroit: Gale Research, 1974.

Smith, Susy. *Prominent American Ghosts*. New York: World Publishing, 1967.

Stein, George, ed. *The Encyclopedia of the Paranormal*. Buffalo: Prometheus, 1996.

Taylor, L. B. *Haunted Virginia: Ghosts and Strange Phenomena of the Old Dominion*. Mechanicsburg, PA: Stackpole Books, 2009.

Taylor, Tim. *The Book of Presidents*. New York: Arno Press, 1972.

Taylor, Troy. *The Haunting of America: Ghosts and Legends from America's Past*. Alton, IL: Whitechapel Productions, 2001.

Thompson, C. J. S. *The Mystery and Lore of Apparitions*. London: Harold Shaylor, 1930.

Truman, Harry. *Memoirs: Years of Trial and Hope*. Garden City, NY: Doubleday, 1956.

Truman, Margaret. *First Ladies*. New York: Random House, 1995.

Wead, Doug. *All the Presidents' Children*. New York: Atria Books, 2003.

Whitcomb, John, and Claire Whitcomb. *Real Life at the White House*. New York: Routledge, 2000.

White House Historical Association. *The White House*. New York: Grosset and Dunlap, 1963.

Whitney, David. *American Presidents*. Garden City, NY: Doubleday, 1978.

## WEB SITES

*The Black Vault*. www.theblackvault.com.

*Ghost Research Society*. www.ghostresearch.org.

Hauck, Dennis William. *White House Ghosts*. www.hauntedplaces.com/WhiteHouseGhosts.htm.

www.legendsofamerica.com/GH-CelebrityGhosts.html

www.whitehouse.gov/about/presidents

# Acknowledgments

This is the tenth book written under the skillful guidance and friendly encouragement of my editor, Kyle Weaver. Brett Keener, Kyle's assistant, demonstrated once again his awesome talents in piloting the manuscript through the production process. My heartfelt thanks to both of them and to the rest of Stackpole's expert staff.

Elizabeth Eckardt once again ably transformed my handwritten, often difficult to decipher manuscript into an intelligible product. She is a paragon of patience and efficiency. Steve Eckardt kept my laptop computer healthy and obedient. Herb Richardson tracked down the books I needed with impressive speed. The friendly and knowledgeable professional librarians at Pitman's McCowan Library and Rowan University's Campbell Library provided invaluable assistance.

I wish to thank the guides and staffs at those presidential homes, museums, and libraries I was fortunate enough to visit, including George Washington's Mount Vernon, Thomas Jefferson's Monticello, James Monroe's Ash Lawn-Highland, Andrew Jackson's Hermitage, James Buchanan's Wheatland, Abraham Lincoln Birthplace National Historic Site, Grover Cleveland Birthplace State Historic Site, Woodrow Wilson Birthplace, the Harding Home, President Calvin Coolidge State Historic Site, Home of Franklin D. Roosevelt National Historic Site, Roosevelt's Little White House Historic Site, Roosevelt's Campobello International Park, Harry S. Truman Library and Museum, Harry S. Truman National Historic Site, Dwight D. Eisenhower Presidential Library and Museum, Eisenhower National Historic Site, and Lyndon B. Johnson National Historical Park.

My lovely wife, Diane, cheerfully accompanied me on our presidential field trips from Vermont to Texas and patiently accepted my untidy office in the home she made beautiful with her presence. Thanks again, my sweetheart.

# About the Author

Charles A. Stansfield Jr. taught geography at Rowan University in Glassboro, New Jersey, for forty-one years and published fifteen textbooks on cultural and regional geography. He is the author of eight titles in the Stackpole Books Haunted Series: *Haunted Arizona, Haunted Northern California, Haunted Southern California, Haunted Ohio, Haunted Vermont, Haunted Maine, Haunted Jersey Shore* and *Haunted New Jersey*.